POLITICS
of
JUGAAD

POLITICS *of* JUGAAD

THE COALITION HANDBOOK

SABA NAQVI

RUPA

Published by
Rupa Publications India Pvt. Ltd 2019
7/16, Ansari Road, Daryaganj
New Delhi 110002

Sales centres:
Allahabad Bengaluru Chennai
Hyderabad Jaipur Kathmandu
Kolkata Mumbai

Copyright © Saba Naqvi 2019

The views and opinions expressed in this book are the author's own and the facts are as reported by her which have been verified to the extent possible, and the publishers are not in any way liable for the same.

All rights reserved.

No part of this publication may be reproduced, transmitted,
or stored in a retrieval system, in any form or by any means,
electronic, mechanical, photocopying, recording or otherwise,
without the prior permission of the publisher.

ISBN: 978-93-5333-418-5

First impression 2019

10 9 8 7 6 5 4 3 2 1

The moral right of the author has been asserted.

Printed by Parksons Graphics Pvt. Ltd, Mumbai

This book is sold subject to the condition that it shall not, by way
of trade or otherwise, be lent, resold, hired out, or otherwise circulated,
without the publisher's prior consent, in any form of binding
or cover other than that in which it is published.

CONTENTS

Introduction: In Praise of Coalitions   1

1. The First Coalition: The Green Shoots   19
2. The Second Coalition: The Short-Lived Janata Experiment   28
3. The Third Coalition: India Emerges Out of Congress Hegemony   34
4. Anti-BJP-ism Replaces Anti-Congressism   44
5. The BJP's Coalition: A True Representation of India's Federal Nature   51
6. The Congress Coalition: From Pro-Poor to Crony Capitalism   64
7. Anna & AAP: The Twilight Phase   76
8. The Arithmetic of the Modi Majority   80
9. The Business of Politics   90
10. Uttar Pradesh: The Coalition Conundrum   100

Epilogue: The Numbers Labyrinth   115

Index   129

Introduction

IN PRAISE OF COALITIONS

The narrative trotted out by many in the mainstream media today makes coalitions sound almost dangerous for the country. The charges are that they are inherently unstable and extractive in nature, implying that smaller players are in a position to blackmail the larger party at the centre of a coalition. Some critiques are valid—we will examine the history of coalitions later in this book—but there is also an exaggerated fear of coalitions. The truth is that many of us have grown up under coalitions—the only thing is we did not perceive it that way. We thought we were under the Manmohan Singh or the Atal Bihari Vajpayee government, identifying a complex regime with a single individual, when, in fact, we have mostly had coalition rule in India since 1989.

A change did take place in 2014, when the Bharatiya Janata Party (BJP) won a simple majority in Parliament. It is since then that the narrative by some sections of the media began to posit single-party rule under a strong leader as the only answer for India. The fascination with a 'great leader', such as Prime Minister (PM) Narendra Modi, is now quite pervasive. The words used for him are 'decisive', 'strong' and an 'individual with authority'. In the past, Indira Gandhi would have fit the same mould.

I started work on this book by looking up the meanings of 'coalesce' and 'coalition'. Briefly, this is what I got from my search. The word 'coalesce', I had imagined, could come from the collision of two objects. However, it means something a little different. According to the *Cambridge Dictionary*, 'coalesce' means to combine into a single group or thing. A coalition, we quite well understand in India, means the joining together of different political parties or groups.

India is the world's second-most populous country and its largest democracy. It is, in a sense, a coalition of states where people speak different languages and have different linguistic and cultural histories. Yet, coalitions somehow have a bad association in some of our minds as being inherently unstable. It is, however, true that in the past, it is only coalitions with a large party as the pivot that have survived their terms. Looking into the future, one can suggest that a mere collection of regional parties is unlikely to survive a term, as the orientation of each constituent would only be towards their region and perhaps not towards the nation as a whole. Still, it is better to recognize that anything can happen and there are no hard and fast rules.

The most common charge levelled at coalitions is that they are bad for governance. But when we examine economic data, it turns out that some of our most prosperous years have been under coalition governments. Being a non-expert on economy, let me refer to others. According to a detailed report published in *The Economics Times* on 29 September 2017, a coalition government that had consensus on policymaking was probably better than the one with a majority, as far as economic growth went. Former Reserve Bank of India (RBI) governor Y.V. Reddy, who headed the institution from 2003 to 2008, told the audience while speaking at the Hudson Institute, a top American think tank in Washington D.C., that since economic liberalization, which began under the premiership of P.V. Narasimha Rao, India's GDP growth rate was the highest in the fiscal year 2007, when it touched 9.6 per cent under the United Progressive Alliance (UPA) led by Manmohan Singh. 'Interestingly, the highest growth in India from 1990 to 2014 was really during coalition governments,' Reddy said. 'So, in a way, it is consensus-based… In [the] Indian situation, a coalition probably produces better economic results than a strong government.' He is not the only individual to have said this—other economists and commentators have noted this too, that coalitions do not suggest poor economic growth.*

Besides, there are other values, such as equality, that

---

*Sruthijith K.K. and Sourabh Gupta, 'Markets are not great at judging how a government will perform: Ruchir Sharma', *The Economic Times*, 7 February 2019, https://economictimes.indiatimes.com/markets/expert-view/markets-are-not-great-at-judging-how-a-government-will-perform-ruchir-sharma/articleshow/67844118.cms

are difficult to measure, which coalitions can bring to the table. In an age where they are also an outcome of very legitimate electoral processes, one can argue that coalitions can be fundamentally more just and representative than single-party regimes. Coalitions give real clout to state parties and thereby to the people of the regions. One could, therefore, argue that, theoretically, the most representative regime that a country like India could have is a coalition of state parties. Take out a hundred-rupee note and look at the picture of Mohandas Karamchand Gandhi on the right; at the centre, '100 rupees' is written in bold, in Hindi; turn the note around, and on the left-hand corner, there is a small column that has '100 rupees' written in fifteen Indian languages.

The currency we handle every day takes note of our extraordinary social composition as a nation: We have several languages with their own scripts and literature (besides the many dialects within the languages).

My question then is this: Why should a party that performs well in the Hindi-speaking parts of India inevitably end up leading the nation? Some of our most significant political leaders have repeatedly got elected from Uttar Pradesh (UP)—Jawaharlal Nehru

(Phulpur), Lal Bahadur Shastri (also from seats around Allahabad), Indira Gandhi (Rae Bareli, though she contested once from Chikmagalur in Karnataka), Rajiv Gandhi (Amethi), Vishwanath Pratap Singh, or V.P. Singh (Allahabad), Chandra Shekhar (Ballia), Sonia Gandhi (Rae Bareli), Vajpayee (Lucknow) and PM Modi (Varanasi). With the exception of Sonia Gandhi, all the others have been PM. H.D. Deve Gowda from Karnataka, Narasimha Rao from Andhra Pradesh and Morarji Desai from Maharashtra also became prime ministers. Manmohan Singh was a Rajya Sabha Member of Parliament (MP) and Inder Kumar Gujral had once contested a Lok Sabha poll from Jalandhar in Punjab.

I have been raised in Delhi, but UP is where my family comes from, scattered across towns in Awadh with an ancestral village in the Rae Bareli district. I love the state and I understand its language, idioms and cultural tones. It has also given me an education on the politics of caste and community. But it is a backward and poor society, and has not made any impressive progress on indices such as health and education. It has also not had any significant economic growth, and joblessness is rampant, as is crime.

Yes, it is the country's most populous state, with a population higher than many large nations'. In 2014, Modi, the former Gujarat chief minister for twelve years, left his home state and stood from the parliamentary seat of Varanasi in UP when he made the successful bid for prime ministership. Varanasi (or Kashi), the holy town by the Ganges, has an all-India symbolism that pervades the consciousness of many Hindus, particularly those from the upper castes. As we head towards the elections in 2019, Ayodhya in UP, not far from my family village, is again being presented as an all-India symbol embodying Lord Ram, in an attempt to create a certain religious-political consciousness.

Yet, it is a valid question for us to ask: In principle, why can we not have a prime minister from Vadodara in Gujarat, the other seat Modi stood from in 2014 and subsequently gave up? Why is it outside the realm of probability that a PM could come from Tamil Nadu or Kerala or the Northeast? Do we believe that a leader who represents the Hindi-speaking regions is more representative of India than those from other regions?

It is, however, states in southern and western India that have far better economic growth. One must wonder if, at some point, other parts of India will resent the sheer political clout of the complex but backward state of UP. This is happening in Europe, where, within nations such as Spain, the more prosperous parts are beginning to resent carrying the can for the rest of the country. But as things stand today, UP will yet again have a big bearing on the 2019 election, as the ruling party, the BJP, got most of its MPs from the state in 2014.

In the 2014 general elections, the BJP won a simple majority with a vote share of 31 per cent in the first-past-the-post system that India follows, because the votes of the Opposition parties were divided. It was one of the more successful conversions of votes to seats in our country's history. The Congress had a dismal showing in 2014, with just 19 per cent of the votes and its lowest tally of 44 seats in Parliament.

But combine the vote shares of the two pre-eminent national parties, and it was 50 per cent. That shows that even in a national election, where people voted for a government at the Centre and not in the states, other parties got the remaining 50 per cent, or half the votes.

There is, therefore, a great legitimacy to our search for a coalition that is truly representative and stable. But there are pitfalls to this exercise due to the competing interests and egos of those who lead political parties.

This book will examine the past even as it looks into the future. It will also examine the processes that make coalitions work and those that make them fail. This book is being written at the cusp of the national election of 2019. Although the BJP, under PM Modi, is technically still a coalition, in the 2014 general elections it also won a simple majority of seats on its own strength, ending a quarter-century of coalition rule.

As we head to the 2019 elections, a coalition remains a possibility. So let's tighten our seat belts and understand the coalition phenomenon in our country. It may be an inevitability we have to live with.

The Cult of 'Absolute' Leadership

When Modi was elected by a simple majority in 2014, I had said that India had shifted on its axis and elected a 'supreme leader' and that the emphatic mandate had ended years of coalition rule. The nation was first given a campaign that was extraordinary in its focus on one man, and then, defying even the most optimistic estimates of his own party, Modi turned the pitch into reality. He created a wave, with the media and advertising acting as force multipliers, and then deftly rode it to a stupendous victory.

Political scientists and commentators had to reboot and think of a new vocabulary and constructs for understanding the dramatic changes in the nation. The cardinal principles of coalitions and consensus so far applied to understanding politics were rendered useless. The cult of 'absolute' leadership, truly a remarkable phenomenon in a nation as large and diverse as India, had to be understood more closely.

Modi's win also came at the cost of utter devastation of the Congress, and Mayawati's Bahujan Samaj Party (BSP), besides a poor showing by Mulayam Singh Yadav's Samajwadi Party (SP), Nitish Kumar's Janata Dal (United), or JD(U), and Lalu Prasad Yadav's Rashtriya Janata Dal (RJD). In 2014, we analysed whether the Modi campaign had overcome traditional caste divisions and whether the process of 'secular' mobilization by a slew of parties would have to be re-examined.

Some of those suppositions turned out to be correct. As his term draws to a close, Modi still emerges in opinion polls as the single-most popular leader. His tenure has also seen the Congress party transform its pitch: It no longer goes for the secular victimhood narrative, and the president of the party, Rahul Gandhi, makes an overt effort to stress his 'Hindu' antecedents by visiting temples, as do party colleagues such as Kamal Nath, recently elected Chief Minister of Madhya Pradesh (who stressed that he would build shelters for cows in each panchayat). These are straws in the wind, but they point to a larger picture.

Although technically still a coalition, the Modi government has given no significant portfolio to any alliance partner; this, is very different from the National Democratic Alliance (NDA) run by Vajpayee. The present condition is altogether a Modi-run show. We have for the past five years known single-party rule, which is stable but with serious questions raised about its economic policies and social agenda.

As we head towards the 2019 polls, there have been setbacks for the BJP in state elections. But it will be the verdict in 2019 that will determine whether people vote differently in state and national polls and whether India's enchantment with a strong leader will prevail over all the disappointments and criticisms.

Modi is a tireless campaigner. In 2014, he addressed

up to five rallies a day, even in far-flung areas where traditional strategists thought the BJP had no chance of winning seats. They were wrong—Modi's instincts were emphatically proven to be right. As he heads into the future, the Modi regime has already begun responding to the Congress pitch as a party of the poor, more concerned with farmers' welfare than the BJP has been. At the beginning of this year, the Congress promised a minimum income for the poor; the Modi regime gave its reply in the last interim budget, announced on 1 February. With sops for farmers and tax benefits for the lower middle class, it was considered a politically smart budget in an election year, although the critical issue of growing joblessness remains unaddressed.

In 2016, the *Oxford Dictionary* chose 'post-truth' as its word of the year. We are living in an age where facts at times seem to matter less than perception and emotions generated over personality and identity. The BJP is good at this. What can also be expected is that in order to hold its bases in UP, the BJP foot soldiers will plan a campaign that will highlight the Hindu-Muslim fault line, focus on the Ram temple and try to tap into or create an apprehension about all rival parties pandering to so-called Muslim interests and vote banks. Evoking the fear of the 'other' is a tried-and-tested formula by right-wing parties across the world. Globally, men and women who emerge as strong right-wing leaders emphasize a certain nationalism underpinned by carefully controlled sectarianism. Such leaders are also seen as agents of dramatic change and, most crucially, as economic reformers. There is, therefore, this unknown element attached to the campaign that the PM will press ahead with. On 14 February, the worst-ever terror attack took place in Pulwama in Kashmir Valley, claiming the lives of 40 CRPF jawans. The subsequent escalating hostilities with Pakistan, plus a crackdown in the Kashmir Valley, is now the backdrop to the 2019 elections.

Across the world, there is demand for assertive, strong leaders who promise to protect 'us' against 'them'. The 'them' is not restricted to just minorities and can include corrupt elites of the past, privileged communities, activists or even the media who are seen as being against the nation in opposing a leader who seeks to identify the nation with his persona.

We would indeed believe we are living in the strongman era if we were to examine what is happening in other countries. Last year, Recep Tayyip Erdoğan was re-elected the president of Turkey in spite of economic decline and growing violence and social divisions during his reign. Erdoğan kept asserting that a strong central authority was needed to guard against terrorism. But Turkey is a country in the middle of the west Asian chaos and war, and we cannot presuppose that the idea of 'fixing terrorists' has equal appeal in India. But this could change in 2019 after the Pulwama attack. Russia's Vladimir Putin, too, is a democratically elected authoritarian leader. In 2019, we will discover whether India just had a passing fancy with an 'absolute leader' or whether it is now a permanent infatuation. We will also discover whether the secular consensus is truly broken, and if India is indeed a nation that asserts the identity of the majority community.

The Opposition's Momentum of Chemistry

The other imponderable is whether the leader of the Congress, Rahul Gandhi, is now taken seriously by the masses and the classes. The Congress has suddenly shown signs of a revival at the end of the Modi term. But only the general elections will give us the answer: Has Rahul Gandhi overcome the years of being dismissed as a lightweight who is not cut out for politics? Actually, after Nehru, every member of the family has been subjected to ridicule. Indira Gandhi was once dismissed as a '*goongi gudiya*' (dumb doll) by her own rivals in the Congress. Sonia Gandhi was the 'foreigner' who delivered speeches in stilted English—but she did have her grand moment of 'sacrifice' when she appointed Manmohan Singh the prime minister of the party in 2004 and was herself president of the party during the decade of the UPA rule. At this time, every member of the grand old party fell at her feet and hailed her as the mother. Rahul, like all the Gandhis before him, is telegenic but hesitant. However, he has been gaining in confidence.

A dramatic twist to India's tryst with the dynasty came on 23 January 2019, when Priyanka Gandhi Vadra was announced the general secretary in charge of eastern UP. The charismatic Gandhi, easy in her campaigning style, has for the first time joined the formal structure of the party. It is a move that can help the Congress even as it creates confusion among non-BJP voters in UP, where the SP and BSP have aligned in an arithmetically significant move to take on the BJP. There is now little possibility of the BSP-SP accommodating the Congress in the arrangement, as they have announced their seats. Either way, Priyanka Gandhi's performance will be tested in the coming months—it can be magnificent or below expectation, but it will certainly add to the drama and colour of the 2019 election.

Priyanka Gandhi's entry was announced at a time when the Congress, after a string of reversals, suddenly tasted success at the end of 2018. But except for the performance in Chhattisgarh, which the Congress won with a large majority, recent gains in Madhya Pradesh and Rajasthan were close. The BJP has strong bases in all the states where it was recently defeated and the party will consciously try to separate state elections from the parliamentary blockbuster. The message it will try to reinforce is: Do you want a chaotic collection of parties or a strong leader who touches each life?

This image has arguably been reinforced by the fact that in the assembly polls, Mayawati put up her own candidates in the states instead of agreeing to the terms of the arrangements offered by the Congress. Her party, the BSP, has small but significant vote banks that are transferable in any alliance. Her actions do not suggest any faith in the Congress, which is anxious to emerge as a coherent national party again after the beating it got in 2014.

Arithmetically, any alliance against the BJP is formidable. But it is still debatable whether such arrangements will get the momentum of chemistry. The Opposition in 2019 will be hoping for the general election to be a sum of the state elections. The BJP will be evoking and defending the record of one leader, who prevailed so magnificently in 2014. It will be doing so in the backdrop of escalating hostility with Pakistan and a crackdown in the Kashmir Valley. Such a stage suits an 'absolute leader'.

What we can say with a level of certainty is that even if Modi's BJP emerges as the single-largest party in 2019, it will probably have to work as a coalition and find partners to either join the government or give outside support. Exactly a decade ago, the Congress surprised itself and the country when it performed better in 2009 after a term in office at the head of UPA-1, showing that anything was possible in Indian politics. But UPA-2 was mired in corruption cases and unseemly controversies, and that is the most recent memory the public has of a Congress-led coalition. This contributed to the party's crash in 2014. In 2019, we will see if voters have forgotten the last few years of UPA-2 and if an association with the new generation of the Nehru-Gandhi dynasty works for the party.

There is also an inherent contradiction in the rise of the Congress and some regional parties, as they are competing, in many instances, for the same voter bases. If we quickly scan the history of coalitions in contemporary India, we will find that regional parties and smaller forces do combine against the dominant party of the age, but when in power, they often do not survive even a term in office.

Chapter 1

THE FIRST COALITION: THE GREEN SHOOTS

The Congress dominated India's politics both at the Centre and at the states for the first two decades after Independence. The year 1967 was significant in the evolution of our democracy as it was the last time that central and state elections were held simultaneously. Thereafter, the calendars in the states stopped matching the Centre's, as regimes fell before their terms were over. It was a process that led us to the present era, where we have very different schedules for state and central elections.

In the first three elections held in India—1952, 1957 and 1962—the Congress won three-fourth of the seats in Parliament and in most states. The most significant defeat came in Kerala in 1957, when the Communist Party of India (CPI) formed the government, the first instance in the world of communism coming through the ballot box, another example of our extraordinarily rich and varied experience with electoral democracy.

What must also be stated is that, in that era, the Congress was boosted by the first-past-the-post system as the BJP is today. In the nation's first general election in 1952, the Congress got 45 per cent of the votes but 74 per cent of the seats. All the non-Congress votes were divided, so political groups such as the socialists of that era failed to record their 10 per cent vote share in seats. (A more recent example of the first-past-the-post system not reflecting voter sentiment with precision can be observed in the 2014 Lok Sabha result, when the BJP converted a 31 per cent vote share to a simple majority; conversely, the BSP got 20 per cent of the votes in UP in 2014 but did not win a single Lok Sabha seat.)

The other significant point about the nature of the Congress in early Independent India is that it actually represented a coalition of interests: It accommodated those who had a rightward tilt both in matters of identity and economy, and also socialists and liberals like Nehru. That gave the party that led the national movement a remarkably elastic nature and the ability to absorb factional fights. It also had, significantly, the ability to represent both the rich and the poor. The nature of the national leadership was that it often came from the English-speaking elite, such as Nehru himself. But the mass movement for Independence also transformed it into a mass party that could represent varied social groups and communities. The Congress was, therefore, in the first two decades of Independent India, omnipotent and omnipresent.

But India's sheer diversity began to throw up challenges for the Congress in the post-Nehru era. First, Nehru died in 1964, and Shastri by consensus became prime minister (the great Congressman from what is now Tamil Nadu, K. Kamaraj, then president of the party, oversaw the process). But Shastri died rather suddenly on a foreign visit in January 1966. The issue of succession now came up in the Congress between

Indira Gandhi and Morarji, who had been chief minister of Bombay state, present-day Maharashtra and Gujarat. Indira Gandhi won that round and became prime minister, but at a time of great economic challenges.

Birth of Anti-Congressism

By 1967, the Congress's grip on absolute power, from the Centre to the states, began to loosen. In the national election held that year, the party, under Indira Gandhi, won a fourth consecutive term in power, but by smaller margins than in the three elections under her father. Price rise, drought, a dip in forex reserves, and protests and strikes by communists and socialists formed the backdrop of the fourth national elections, when states voted simultaneously.

A significant figure of that age was socialist leader Ram Manohar Lohia, whose contribution to the political ideas that have shaped our country's history has perhaps not got its due recognition. He was a freedom fighter and one-time member of the Congress who became deeply critical of Nehru. He developed several radical ideas about caste, class and what can be called socialist theory applicable to a once-colonized nation like India. He gave multiple political ideas in his writings. He began to see the Congress as inimical to the interests of the people of India. He died young at the age of 57 in 1967, but it was he who had, in principle, advocated the coming together of parties of different ideologies to defeat a common foe. He coined the phrase 'anti-Congressism'. This is relevant today, as the idea of disparate forces coming together to take down a common foe is one of the primary impulses that drive coalition politics. The difference is that from anti-Congressism, we have moved to anti-BJP-ism as being the impulse behind the process.

But back to 1967, which would turn out to be a watershed in the history of challenges presented to the Congress. As we have noted, the Congress under Indira Gandhi managed power at the Centre. But the party lost seven states in one fell swoop. New players emerged on the political landscape, most significantly the Dravida Munnetra Kazhagam (DMK) in Madras state, now Tamil Nadu, after leading an anti-Hindi agitation. The other states where the Congress lost power were UP, Haryana, Punjab, Bihar, Madhya Pradesh, Orissa (now Odisha) and West Bengal.

To be able to replace the Congress in some of these

states, coalitions began to be forged between ideologically incongruent forces. Simultaneously, the process of splits and defections began. In UP, for instance, Jat leader Charan Singh left the Congress with a chunk of its Members of the Legislative Assembly (MLAs) to become chief minister, supported by non-Congress parties. The Swatantra Party also made an appearance at this time. Founded by C. Rajagopalachari in 1959, the party was opposed to land ceilings, cooperative farming and the economic policies being pursued by Nehru's Congress. Winning seats in Rajasthan, Gujarat and Orissa, it got 44 MPs with almost 9.6 per cent of the votes polled—it had emerged as the single-largest Opposition party in the Lok Sabha. Yet, it was not declared the official Opposition in the Lok Sabha, as it was short by some seats to get the required 10 per cent. (Similarly, after the 2014 verdict, the Congress did not have the numbers to get the constitutional perks of an official Opposition party.)

In 1967, the Swatantra Party did play a part in forming ideologically disparate coalitions in the states. The party attracted landlords, feudals and former princes but did not survive the long haul in terms of ideas. Today, I would describe it as an interest group of liberals who wished to pursue right-wing economic policies.

But the more significant role in forming coalitions driven by anti-Congressism was played by the socialists, who were also putting Lohia's ideas to the test. It is in this year that the coalition regime in Bihar included two socialist parties, the Bharatiya Jana Sangh, or the Jana Sangh (precursor to the BJP), and the CPI. Similarly, a regime in Punjab combined Akali groups, communists, socialists and, again, the Jana Sangh.

These state regimes did not last long, but a process had been started. (Although the BJP was founded in 1980, it would be a mistake to see its history as beginning then. The Jana Sangh, the political wing of the Rashtriya Swayamsevak Sangh, or the RSS, was active in coalitions from the time the parties got together against the Congress.)

The coalition of anti-Congress forces consisting of many shades of socialists and the Jana Sangh, along with the Swatantra Party bunch, soon frittered away their opportunities. But there was a Congress split in December 1969, when Indira Gandhi fell out with the old guard of the Congress, referred to as the Syndicate and called the Congress (O). She called for early elections in 1971, when again the old Lohia strategy of 'all against the Congress' was put to the test. This was called the Grand Alliance and included parties across the spectrum, except the left parties. The various factions of the socialist parties, the Jana Sangh, the Swatantra Party and a few others, joined forces.

This is when Indira Gandhi showed her mettle as a ruthless and shrewd politician. The process of what is now known as populism worked for her, as she shifted politics more leftwards and came up with the *'Garibi hatao'* (remove poverty) slogan (it was her response to the 'Indira hatao' [remove Indira] slogan coined by the Opposition). The coalition was temporarily crushed—as was the Congress (O), which won just 16 seats compared to the 375 won by Indira Gandhi's Congress (called Congress-R, which stood for Requisitionists, quite a complex word for a political party). Indira Gandhi, with her personality, legacy and pro-poor sloganeering, had re-established the dominance of the Congress. She had bettered her father's record of winning seats. The Grand Alliance won under 40 seats.

But one more pointer to the future had emerged in 1971: The communists had supported Congress (R).

In doing so, they began the tradition of supporting the Congress at the Centre while fighting them in state bastions like Kerala and West Bengal.

Chapter 2

THE SECOND COALITION: THE SHORT-LIVED JANATA EXPERIMENT

By all accounts, 1971 was a great year for Indira Gandhi. She had become the champion of the poor (by then she had also abolished the privy purses of former feudals and had nationalized banks). By the end of that year, even a Jana Sangh MP such as Vajpayee compared her to a goddess: This came after the Indian Army intervened in the West and East Pakistan conflict, and India played a role in the formation of Bangladesh. Indira Gandhi was both a heroine of the poor and of the war.

The Congress, led by her, swept through the state elections of 1972 (she had forwarded the national election of 1971 by a year). But this phenomenal victory hid the seeds of destruction that lay within it. By now, the Congress was a party under a 'supreme leader' and not an elastic and democratic coalition of interests with multiple power centres. Many commentators say that the BJP has undergone a similar change after 2014.

There was also a price to pay for the war with Pakistan that took place in 1971–72. The economy was jolted by the costs of war, the 8 million Bangladeshi refugees who streamed into India and the decision of the United States (US) to stop aid to India after the war. The years 1973 and 1974 witnessed some of the highest inflations, of 23–30 per cent. The monsoons failed in 1972–73 and the agriculture sector was in distress, even as industrial growth was low. Political forces harnessed the dissatisfaction that raged in huge protests. Two states in particular—Gujarat and Bihar—both Congress-ruled, led. Students were at the forefront of both, which first came up against spiralling prices and then became about overall discontent and searching for an alternative.

In Bihar, the movement found a leader in the old socialist Lok Nayak Jayaprakash Narayan, also called JP, who demanded the dismissal of the Congress government and sounded the call for what he called 'total revolution'. In Gujarat, the old Indira Gandhi foe, Congressman Morarji, who had opposed her after the death of Shastri, went on a fast. The students pressed for fresh elections, and the Congress was defeated.

The backdrop to all these agitations was also the great general strike in the Indian Railways, then led by the late George Fernandes, who was then a trade union activist but would, decades later, play a big role in enabling a coalition for the BJP. But back then, all alliances were driven by anti-Congressism. In 1975, JP led one of the biggest marches seen in the national capital to Parliament. The socialists, the Jana Sangh and the Congress (O) began to project him as an alternative to Indira Gandhi. The prime minister, meanwhile, clung to power and, pushed to a corner, imposed on India one of its darkest periods.

With the aim of putting off the general elections due in early 1976, and of crushing the Opposition,

Indira Gandhi imposed the Emergency on India. This dark chapter began on 25 June 1975. Civil liberties were suspended, protests and strikes were banned, Opposition leaders and students leading protests were sent to jail, and newspapers were subjected to censorship. The Emergency lasted about one and a half years and was lifted on 18 January 1977, when the government announced fresh elections. But we should never forget how close we came to losing our great journey with democracy.

The Opposition Unites and Then Fails

Indira Gandhi must have imagined she had crushed the Opposition. But the various Opposition parties came together quickly to form the altogether new Janata Party. Anyone opposed to the Emergency, even from within the Congress, joined the party. Notable among them was Jagjivan Ram, one of the most prominent Dalit leaders thrown up by electoral democracy. The Jana Sangh formally ceased to exist, as it merged its identity with the new party. But the most prominent were the socialists and the Lok Dal of Charan Singh, which also merged with the Janata Party. All of them accepted the leadership of JP, and the main aim of their campaign was to oppose Indira Gandhi and the Emergency.

The results of the 1977 election became the first electoral defeat recorded by the Congress—and it came three decades after Independence. The Janata Party and its allies won 330 of the 542 seats in Parliament; the Congress fell to 154.

But the Janata Party experiment is a lesson on how not to run a government based on a coalition of political forces. The main issue that marred its politics was the ego tussle between three prime ministerial candidates—Morarji, Charan Singh and Jagjivan Ram. Morarji was the first PM, but eighteen months later, the Janata regime lost its majority when Charan Singh pulled out—incredibly, with the support of the Congress. Four months later, the Congress pulled the plug on him, and it was back to elections.

As far as coalitions go, this was a truly bad model, in which ego battles were the primary concern and there was no common programme or slogan beyond defeating a particular force. No alternative programme of governance emerged and the regime was bereft of any ideas beyond defeating Indira Gandhi.

The diverse political and ideological orientation of the constituents of the Janata regime suggests that it was, in a sense, a repeat of the anti-Congress unity visible a decade ago in 1967 in the states. Both were destined to fail. In the 1980 election, the Congress was back with a bang, with 343 seats, and the Janata Party was all but finished. Its offshoots would later emerge in states under specific leaders and play a more lasting role in transforming politics, but another dramatic decade would elapse before all that could happen.

Chapter 3

THE THIRD COALITION: INDIA EMERGES OUT OF CONGRESS HEGEMONY

Indira Gandhi was assassinated in 1984, following which her son Rajiv Gandhi, then a novice in politics, received the largest mandate in India's history. The Congress won 411 out of 542 seats and was in office until 1989. But at the end of this term, the Congress lost the national elections. This was the year in which the Congress domination in Indian politics ended.

New social and political forces reshaped Indian politics. First, the old Jana Sangh ceased to exist when it merged into the Janata Party. A new party—the BJP—was founded in 1980 with veteran Jana Sangh parliamentarian Vajpayee as its first president. In the 1984 election, held after Indira Gandhi's assassination, this young party was reduced to 2 seats, with Vajpayee himself facing a humiliating defeat from Gwalior to Madhavrao Scindia (father of present Congress leader Jyotiraditya Scindia).

Second, Rajiv Gandhi's prime ministership ended on a controversial note on the issue of the government allegedly taking large kickbacks in purchasing Bofors guns from Sweden. This became one of the biggest defence scandals to impact political fortunes. A significant political player of this age who deserves mention in any work on coalitions is V.P. Singh. He was an old-school Congressman who had worked with Indira Gandhi and had been appointed chief minister of UP by her in 1980 after she was re-elected when the Janata experiment failed. Rajiv Gandhi turned to this man, who had a reputation for integrity and for being a tough administrator, to run his finance ministry and begin the process of opening up the Indian economy.

V.P. Singh was a finance minister who oversaw the relaxation of the regulated economy referred to as the 'licence raj'. But he was also tough on corruption, and it was always suggested that he was looking into any big business that allegedly funded the Congress generously. During V.P. Singh's reign at the finance ministry, income tax raids took place on Dhirubhai Ambani (the founder of the Reliance empire) and film star Amitabh Bachchan, then a great friend of the Gandhi family.

V.P. Singh was therefore shifted to the Ministry of Defence, which turned out to be a terrible idea by the Rajiv Gandhi government. There he began to look into corruption in defence procurements, such as the Howaldtswerke-Deutsche Werft GmbH (HDW) submarine and the Bofors deal. Before he could initiate an investigation, he was dismissed from the Cabinet and subsequently resigned from the Congress party. He first formed an outfit known as the Jana Morcha and was then re-elected to the Lok Sabha in a by-election from Allahabad. Next, in October 1988, another party bearing the 'Janata' name came into being, now called the Janata Dal, with V.P. Singh as president. It merged with the Jana Morcha, the various offshoots of the

Janata Party, the Lok Dal led by Charan Singh and a splinter of the Congress known as the Congress (S).

Non-Congress Actors Set the Narrative

What followed was more significant in terms of understanding the growing heft of regional parties. The Janata Dal came to an understanding with state-specific parties such as the DMK in Tamil Nadu, the Telugu Desam Party (TDP) in Andhra Pradesh, then led by cinema idol N.T. Rama Rao (N.T.R.), and the Asom Gana Parishad (AGP) in Assam. N.T.R. was president and V.P. Singh the convener of this National Front, as it was called.

The second step in the process of getting the better of the Congress was to come to an understanding with both the Right and the Left of Indian politics, namely the BJP and the communist parties, the latter by now split into two significant factions.

The National Front was working on the principle that a divided Opposition vote would benefit the Congress, thereby going on to have a loose understanding with various forces in their respective areas of strength. For instance, in about 80 per cent of seats where both had some support, the BJP and the National Front did not contest against each other. Similarly, candidates were not put up in regions where communists had their bases.

The result of the 1989 election revealed a new pattern for an India emerging out of Congress hegemony. The Congress would still emerge as the single-largest party, with 197 seats in the House of 543. The National Front had fewer—146 seats—but it got the support of the BJP, which had 86 seats, and the left parties, which had fifty-two. Both the BJP and the Left were, however, giving outside support and were not part of the government.

V.P. Singh became PM on 2 December 1989. He did not even last a year in the PM's chair, but unleashed forces that would permanently transform Indian politics. First, a few months after the V.P. Singh government took charge in Delhi, the Janata Dal came to power in several Indian states. This marked the birth of state-specific forces that held their bases, sometimes in power, sometimes in Opposition. Biju Patnaik, for instance, won in Orissa on the Janata Dal symbol—the beginning of the challenge to the Congress in the state that has now been ruled for three terms by his son Naveen Patnaik (the party is now called the Biju Janata Dal, or the BJD).

Mulayam and Lalu came to power in UP and Bihar, respectively, as Janata Dal leaders and are both still running significant parties whose nomenclatures have changed even as state dynasties have been created. Mulayam's party, now led by his son Akhilesh Yadav, is the SP, while Lalu's party, also led by a son, Tejashwi Yadav, is the RJD. In the state elections of 1990, the Janata Dal also emerged in Gujarat under Chimanbhai Patel, and in Haryana under Om Prakash Chautala. Constituents of the National Front, meanwhile, also came to power in Andhra Pradesh (TDP) and Assam (AGP).

Indian politics was changing, and in the middle of these swirling waters, V.P. Singh, himself an upper-caste Thakur from a small principality in UP, implemented the Mandal Commission report. The Mandal Commission had been established in 1979 by the Janata Party government under a parliamentarian named B.P. Mandal to identify 'the socially and economically backward classes of India' and to consider extending reservation to them. Since the Other Backward Classes (OBCs) made up 52 per cent of the population, the commission recommended that OBCs be granted 27 per cent of jobs in government and public sector undertakings, thereby taking the reservation to 49 per cent (as Scheduled Tribes [STs] and Scheduled Castes [SCs] already had reservation).

The report had been sitting in cold storage since its submission in 1983. Then, on his Independence Day address on 15 August 1990, V.P. Singh declared the intention of implementing the Mandal Commission report and set the cat among the pigeons. Large-scale student protests broke out among the forward castes, but no party that depended on popular mandates could afford to openly take positions against a decision that appeared to empower the largest caste bloc in Indian society.

Mandal, therefore, forever transformed politics in northern India as OBCs were empowered and parties drawing from subaltern power, such as the BSP (besides the various avatars of the Janata Dal), developed almost permanent voter blocs drawn on caste. Parties such as the Congress and the BJP that had a tradition of upper castes in leadership roles struggled to come to terms with the new reality. (The Congress has still not recovered in UP and Bihar.)

The BJP struck back with its own brand of agitational politics, which eventually led to the collapse of the V.P. Singh government. By the time the party gave outside support to the National Front, the BJP had already passed what came to be known as the Palampur resolution (passed at the meeting of the party's national executive in the town of Palampur in Himachal Pradesh), declaring its intention of joining an agitation run by the Vishva Hindu Parishad (VHP) to demand a Ram temple at Ayodhya in place of the Babri Masjid, which then stood at the spot. It was at the time a statement of intent.

On 25 September 1990, BJP leader Lal Krishna Advani started a rath yatra from Somnath to Ayodhya to press for a Ram mandir. He claimed he was headed to Ayodhya to offer *kar seva* to build a temple. The journey lit a divisive trail along its path. On 23 October 1990, Lalu, then chief minister of Bihar, arrested Advani in Bihar's Samastipur district. The BJP withdrew support to the V.P. Singh government, and it fell.

Notably, in 1990, non-Congress actors were setting the narrative. That era is usually described as 'Mandal versus Mandir', and the forces behind both were to go on to establish themselves as long-term players in politics. The Hindutva form of agitational identity politics had arrived; simultaneously, in the two significant Hindi heartland states of UP and Bihar, upper-caste hegemony was being challenged as never before, and each of these states would eventually have caste-based parties with regional variations.

The Congress started playing back-room games. One hand was played immediately after V.P. Singh lost the support of the BJP. His big rival in the Janata Dal had been socialist leader Chandra Shekhar, who believed he had been deprived of the PM's post in 1989. Now he broke away from the main Janata Dal with a group of followers and became prime minister with the support of the Congress. He lasted seven months before the Congress pulled the plug on him and the country headed towards another election.

Let's remember that the Congress had done something similar a decade earlier, when Charan Singh had replaced Morarji as PM during the Janata Party era. Charan Singh's party, the Lok Dal, too, came loosely from the socialist tradition. But as would happen with Lalu in Bihar and Mulayam in UP, his party settled into dynastic succession. Now called the Rashtriya Lok Dal (RLD), Charan Singh's grandson Jayant Chaudhary and son Ajit Singh still have a following among the Jats of western UP and are junior partners in the alliance that BSP and SP have announced.

Charan Singh was PM for four months and Chandra Shekhar for seven months before the Congress withdrew support. Both had campaigned against the Congress but did not hesitate to take its support to get ahead of their rivals within the coalition fronts. So when we refer to ego battles extracting their price on coalition politics, these two are good examples. But as we enter the 1990s, we see that certain trends have been established. The National Front experiment can also be seen as the first instance of a Third Front formation coming to power—a coalition of parties from the states, with national parties only playing an outside role.

Chapter 4

ANTI-BJP-ISM REPLACES ANTI-CONGRESSISM

Sixteen months after the 1989 election, the country was headed towards another general election in 1991. India had now entered an age when coalitions were all it had to work with. Until 2014, no party would get a simple majority in Parliament. Mandal and mandir were the big issues in north India as the country headed towards voting day in 1991. On the one hand, riots had broken out and religious polarization was spreading. Simultaneously, subaltern mobilization was taking place along caste lines, triggering acute upper-caste resentment in north India.

Then came a big tragedy. On 21 May 1991, after one round of voting, Rajiv Gandhi was assassinated while campaigning in Tamil Nadu. He was blown to bits by a human bomb, the second member of India's first family to meet a brutal end—his mother had been killed by her own Sikh security guards, and he was assassinated by the Liberation Tigers of Tamil Eelam (LTTE) of Sri Lanka, giving an idea of the other big battles being fought in the backdrop of our ever-moving electoral engine. The tragedy cast a shadow on the polls, but they continued after a delay.

Indira Gandhi's assassination had resulted in a huge sympathy wave from the electorate and the Congress had secured its highest number of seats in history. Now Rajiv Gandhi's assassination resulted in a clear divergence, if we examine the results from where the polls were held before he was killed and where the elections took place thereafter. The Congress did far better post assassination and emerged as the single-largest party with 244 seats. The BJP had 120, its highest ever, indicating that the

Ram mandir movement had put it on a growth trajectory. The Janata Dal had 69.

The Congress formed a minority government with the support of the All India Anna Dravida Munnetra Kazhagam (AIADMK) and some smaller parties. Narasimha Rao, a veteran, was pulled out of virtual retirement and made prime minister, and his government completed a full term in office. There were, however, convulsions when the Babri mosque was demolished on 6 December 1992. By then, the BJP had come to power in four states and their governments in UP, Madhya Pradesh, Himachal Pradesh and Rajasthan were dismissed by the Centre after the demolition.

In the next general election of 1996, the Congress was no longer the single-largest party in India. This election delivered a fractured mandate, but the BJP was the single-largest party, with 161 MPs in a House of 543. The Congress had twenty-one fewer MPs, with 140 seats.

Another experiment in coalition politics began: The same social and political forces that had put together the National Front in 1989 now came together to create what was called the United Front in 1996.

This unity, however, marked a distinct break with the past. It was unity against the BJP, whose earlier avatar, the Jana Sangh, was part of the political combines, in one way or another, since 1967, when coalitions began to come together to challenge the Congress.

What is interesting about the short-lived United Front experiment is that it was driven by the logic of keeping the BJP out of power. So we can say that this was an instance of anti-BJP-ism replacing anti-Congressism. It, therefore, appears to be an impulse in Indian politics that regional forces come together against the dominant party of the age—which, for most of Independent India's history, was the Congress, but today is the BJP.

Another Experiment in Third Front Politics

By now we have seen different coalition models tried out in India, including a collection of regional parties supported from outside by a national party such as the Congress. The best example of this kind of coalition is that of thirteen parties which came together to form the United Front government in 1996. It was a minority government that survived at the mercy of the Congress, which played a part in both making and breaking that coalition.

The BJP got the first chance at government formation under Vajpayee but failed to muster the support of regional parties, and Vajpayee resigned in thirteen days. That is when the United Front was put together, a strategy that the Congress and the Communist Party of India (Marxist), or CPI(M), worked out together. This is, therefore, also an instance of the communists working with the Congress, as they have always seen the right-wing forces, such as the BJP, as the greater enemy.

And so the United Front was born, again an experiment in Third Front politics. Karnataka politician Deve Gowda, a prominent Janata Dal leader in his home state but unknown outside, was the unexpected choice to be prime minister with outside support of the Congress. In June 1996, the government was sworn in, but less than a year later, the Congress forced a leadership change and Gujral, less rooted in mass politics than Deve Gowda but also from the Janata Dal and a former MP from Jalandhar in Punjab, became PM. His tenure lasted about a month longer than Deve Gowda's, before the Congress again pulled the plug on him. This time, the Congress had demanded that Gujral remove DMK ministers from the government. By then, the Jain Commission report looking into the had assassination of Rajiv Gandhi had held that members of the DMK had tacitly supported those who had assassinated the former PM, although it failed to establish direct complicity. Gujral refused and the Congress brought down his government.

It must be noted that this was an interim phase in the history of the Congress. After Narasimha Rao finished his term as PM and Congress president, he was replaced by Sitaram Kesri, an OBC leader from Bihar (possibly a response to the Mandalization of politics). Kesri was president during 1996–98, a brief phase in the history of the party that was now wedded to dynastic politics. The process of persuading Rajiv Gandhi's widow, Sonia Gandhi, to take charge of the party was ongoing throughout Kesri's tenure, and the former eventually took charge in 1998. Sonia Gandhi remained at the helm of party affairs for nearly two decades, until December 2017, when her son Rahul Gandhi replaced her.

Politically, the Congress confronted a genuine problem in supporting the United Front, as it was the compulsions of a hung house. The Congress was being compelled to empower forces that had eaten into its bases. There was, therefore, an inbuilt contradiction in the entire arrangement of the party giving support to the Deve Gowda and the Gujral regimes. When it came to the forces of the Janata parivar, which had by now acquired distinct regional identities, the Congress was supporting those who had taken over its voter blocs. It was being forced to appear to be friends with the Janata parivar at the Centre even as it was being challenged by them in the states.

One can, therefore, say that the Congress never intended to give too much oxygen to the Third Front arrangement—it was just waiting for the time and opportunity to establish its primacy again, failing which it settled for a brief interregnum of playing back-room games. Eventually, the Congress withdrew support and the country headed towards another general election in 1998. But the Congress did not gain from this—the BJP did.

Chapter 5

THE BJP'S COALITION: A TRUE REPRESENTATION OF INDIA'S FEDERAL NATURE

The BJP created the template for the first successful coalition regime under the leadership of Vajpayee. There were two models of coalitions led by him—the 1998 government that collapsed in a year, which was a post-poll coming together of forces to muster a simple majority, and the 1999 regime that lasted its entire term till 2004, which involved prepoll arrangements. In both cases, the BJP sat down and hammered out a Common Minimum Programme (CMP) with its allies.

What had by then become clear was that one or the other of the 'national' parties was needed to anchor a coalition, as the potential Third Front never had adequate numbers. The Congress had by then played too many toppling games with Third Front arrangements, and the party was seen as being in decline. The BJP was growing and, under Vajpayee, the party set out intelligently to present a moderate face and thereby attract allies.

First, a quick background. As we have seen, the predecessor of the BJP, the Jana Sangh, played a role in creating alternatives to the Congress from the very beginning, when coalitions emerged in states in 1967. The Jana Sangh was founded in 1951 by Shyama Prasad Mukherjee and existed as a political party until 1977 without any ambiguity about its being the political project of the RSS. In 1977, it merged with several other parties, ideologically Left, Right and Centrist, which were opposed to the Congress in the post-Emergency era, and the Janata Party was born. One of the reasons for the former Jana Sangh members' break with the Janata Party was also the socialists raising the issue of their 'dual membership' as they also swore allegiance to the RSS. Eventually, the BJP, with Vajpayee as its first president, was formed in 1980.

In his presidential address, Vajpayee played down the RSS and the Jana Sangh connection and, instead, focused on the legacy of JP, the socialist leader. He himself was inclined to a moderate path, but the party was faced with a near rout in 1984 and that is when the BJP returned to its basic ideology and began the process of rebuilding its core by playing the Hindu card. This culminated in the Ayodhya movement, which would transform politics and signal the arrival of the BJP as a national player.

Yet, after the demolition of the Babri mosque in December 1992, the same Advani who had led the Ram temple movement came to believe that India could not be conquered by stridency alone. After 1993, the search for allies and the incremental vote began. Advani, the architect of the revival, himself believed a more moderate image was now needed to be projected. The party, therefore, decided to build a remarkably successful personality-oriented campaign around Vajpayee. His long record as a parliamentarian stood him in good stead, besides friendships and respect across the political spectrum.

Contrary to what we have seen happening in the coalition interregnums, where ego battles resulted in leaders undermining one another, we saw something different in the BJP. For all their differences, at a strategically significant time, Advani, the creator of the new vibrant BJP, was willing to step aside as Vajpayee came forward.

Having covered that era, I noticed there was an irony in the BJP's scramble for alliance partners. During the 1998 campaign, Vajpayee would attack the preceding United Front coalition with these lines: *'Kahin ka eent, kahin ka roda, Bhanumati ne kunba joda* [a brick from here, a brick from there, that's how Bhanumati got her flock together].' It was a line that always got a response from the crowds in the Hindi heartland. Now the BJP was doing the same, but they would make it work.

The Vajpayee Era—a Milestone in the BJP's Journey

As a young reporter, I had covered Vajpayee's swearing in in 1998. It was a big transitional moment in Indian politics. It was as much about the BJP and Vajpayee as it was about sensible coalition formation. Those who scripted the first regime of the BJP included socialist Fernandes. He was a central pivot in the National Democratic Alliance, or NDA, as it came to be known.

The presence of regional forces in the Vajpayee dispensation must be stressed. Besides the BJP contingent, sworn in on that day too was Ramakrishna Hegde, former Janata Party leader and the first non-Congress chief minister of Karnataka. Also sworn in was another former chief minister, this time of Punjab, and leader of the Shiromani Akali Dal (SAD), Surjit Singh Barnala. Two junior ministers who took oath were Nitish Kumar and Naveen Patnaik—both would go on to serve multiple terms as chief ministers of their respective states, Bihar and Odisha. In the next NDA under Vajpayee formed a year later, current West Bengal Chief Minister Mamata Banerjee, too, was sworn in, unbelievable as it may sound today. She had not yet defeated the communists in the state and was charting an identity separate from the party to which she had originally belonged—the Congress.

The ceremony that I had the privilege of witnessing was, therefore, a landmark moment in politics. Beyond the importance of a BJP leader becoming prime minister, regional forces of the past and the future were very much part of this experiment in coalition formation.

There are various levels on which 1998 turned out to be significant. For instance, in the realm of political strategy, what the BJP did was noteworthy: The same party that had spearheaded the Ram temple agitation had somehow managed to take positions that sought to consciously blunt the counter polarization. This was directed not so much at vote banks that would remain inimical to them but at alliance partners. In this project, the party was mostly successful. We can, therefore, state that the calibration of its ideology was a feature of the BJP's rise, as the Vajpayee era was fundamentally about coalitions.

There was, however, an inherent fault line in the 1998 coalition: It was put together by getting letters of support from smaller parties. This meant that after the results came in, political parties scrambled to connect and get the numbers required for government formation. Since no party had a simple majority, it was necessary for any potential front to give letters of support to the president before the leader of the front could be invited to form a government.

Various parties stepped up. A significant player was TDP leader Chandrababu Naidu, then chief minister of undivided Andhra Pradesh. The party founded by his father-in-law N.T.R. had always played an important role in coalition formation, and this time too, the TDP was not going to be left out. Chandrababu was then still negotiating the secularism question and hence chose to give outside support to the Vajpayee dispensation. This meant that the TDP would not participate in the government but wouldn't pull it down either. This also meant that he could extract many lucrative deals for the party and state even as it did not have to answer questions or own up to any responsibility, in case the script went awry.

More drama ensued with another party from the south of India. The first Tamil Nadu-based ally that Vajpayee got in 1998 was the AIADMK, led by the late J. Jayalalithaa, which was out of power in the state but had eighteen MPs. Jayalalithaa would join the government, but not before tormenting Vajpayee over the required letter of support. Indeed, the weakness in the new government could be seen in its very foundation. All the allies sent their letters of support to then president K.R. Narayanan by

12 March 1998. But Jayalalithaa made them wait for another forty-eight hours—and those were tense moments.

The letter eventually came, but Jayalalithaa would make a difficult ally and eventually play her part in bringing down the government, leading to another election in 1999. The government would fall by one vote in Parliament during a confidence vote after Jayalalithaa would withdraw support.

But this actually proved to be a blessing in disguise for the NDA, which went to the next stage by fighting as a pre-election alliance and winning a comfortable majority. What was attempted in 1999 really marked the coming of age of the coalition model. After the 1998 tumble, what BJP leaders and figures such as Fernandes managed to put together was a pre-election alliance of twenty-four parties. This meant that members of the alliance did not contest against each other and the BJP fought for a fewer number of seats, although its leader, Vajpayee, was again pitched as the prime ministerial face.

But there was another organic process at work in this arrangement. The federal nature of the Indian republic was stressed; regional parties were given seats at the high table and treated as equal partners by Vajpayee. In this enterprise, I believe that the personality of the figures that dominated the BJP of that age mattered. In spirit, Vajpayee was a democrat who respected India's parliamentary traditions. He was not out to control every department and realm of government. His personality was, therefore, an element in the success of the BJP's coalition.

There were, in addition, new impulses that were now brought into the political realm. Each of the constituents of the NDA had its own vote bank in the states, in some cases the lower castes and even a section of minority communities. They, therefore, brought both a regional and a caste sensibility to the government in Delhi. They can also be seen as a moderating influence on the Vajpayee regime, which lasted a full term, until 2004.

After events such as the Gujarat riots of 2002 took place, the alliance partners complained that these became factors in their defeat in the state elections that followed in 2004. Briefly, the BJP's ideologically hardline positions and actions damaged the alliance partners (with the exception of the Shiv Sena in Maharashtra), while moderate positions helped them hold their diverse vote banks.

At the outset, the BJP had agreed to a CMP that excluded three promises in the party's election manifesto. It was stated clearly that these three issues were off the table for a coalition: the construction of a Ram temple at Ayodhya, the enactment of a uniform civil code in India and the abolition of Article 370 of the Indian Constitution that gives special constitutional rights to the state of Jammu and Kashmir (J&K).

It was not as if the BJP prime minister gave up the demand for a Ram temple. Whenever Vajpayee felt cornered by the hardliners in his government and the ideological family of the RSS, he would make remarks about the temple. The allies would go rushing to him saying it was off the agenda, and then he would turn around and tell his ideological fraternity that his hands were tied by the 'dharma' of coalition politics!

There was also a National Agenda for Governance that was put together with inputs from all the parties in 1999. The preamble of this agenda clearly stated that 'with consensus on common cause and common set of principles, the constituents of the NDA sunk differences to weld into a solid phalanx of a single dominant political formation and thereby fulfilled the resolve of the Indian people to give themselves a stable, strong and progressive government'. The word 'progressive' certainly suggests that Fernandes, who went on to become the defence minister, had a big hand in working this out.

If we examine the electoral strength of the BJP in the three elections in 1996, 1998 and 1999, there is only a 21-seat growth. In 1996, the BJP was the single-largest party in Parliament with 161 seats, but its allies were limited, such as the ideologically compatible Shiv Sena with its bases in Maharashtra. In 1998, the BJP had 179 seats and the allies who agreed to support it had 72; the Congress had 141 seats. In 1999, when the BJP went for a pre-election alliance with multiple parties, its own seats only increased by three to 182, but the score of NDA allies went up to 100 and that of the Congress dipped to its lowest until that point—a meagre 114 seats.

But there was a journey made between 1996, when Vajpayee resigned after thirteen days as head of state, and 1999, when a coalition could look stable. The BJP was the first party in India's history to lead a coalition that would survive an entire term. What must also be stated is that parties that joined the first BJP government at the Centre simultaneously prospered in the states, as the national partner was not threatening to take over their bases. As we have seen, figures such as Nitish Kumar, Naveen Patnaik and Mamata Banerjee went on to become mighty state satraps, and that being part of the Vajpayee establishment was a stepping stone in their individual journeys.

During the Vajpayee era, a successful alliance model for Bihar was also worked out to challenge Lalu's power. Nitish Kumar and Fernandes began the tradition of entering into state-specific alliances with the BJP for the assembly elections as well. What this meant was that both partners in the alliance were beneficiaries of the arrangement.

In conclusion, we can say that the NDA coalition was truly representative of the federal nature of India. Vajpayee's six-year reign was a milestone in the BJP's journey to becoming India's pre-eminent political party. He presided over that significant time in contemporary Indian history when the BJP ended what was called its 'untouchability'. It was Vajpayee's reputation and personal conduct that made it possible for regional parties to flock to the BJP. In the future, whenever strategy or politics requires the BJP to appear gentler and kinder, it can just revisit the legacy of its first prime minister.

But the BJP became be a very different party in its next avatar in power. After 2014, the next NDA coalition in spirit was actually an assertion of single-party rule, although technically it was still an alliance. Allies are not significant to the BJP now, led by PM Modi and party president Amit Shah. That is why even an ideologically similar party such as the Shiv Sena has problems with the BJP today—unlike what happened in the Vajpayee era—as the BJP is also eating into the bases of its alliance partner in Maharashtra. Meanwhile, the TDP has exited the Modi-led NDA, as have smaller parties in Bihar and the AGP in Assam. Nitish Kumar, Chief Minister of Bihar, has acted erratically since Modi's 2014 win, first leaving the NDA in 2013 and then rejoining it in 2017. Broadly, regional and state parties make alliances and stick with them only if their self-interests are served.

Chapter 6

THE CONGRESS COALITION: FROM PRO-POOR TO CRONY CAPITALISM

By the time the country headed for the 2004 election, the Congress party had learnt to cope with the era of coalitions and had some tactical understanding with regional forces on the ground, while the BJP fought as the NDA. What was also significant about the 2004 polls is that the BJP did not fight on ideological or Hindutva issues—it pitched its economic performance and projected that 'India was shining' under its watch.

In the end, the BJP was stunned when it got 7 seats less than the Congress. The BJP went down from 182 in 1999 to 138, a loss of 44 seats. The Congress went up from 114 in 1999 to 145, a gain of 31 seats. There was not much of a difference in the tally of the two parties that claimed to be 'national', but what hit the NDA hard was not just the main party's numbers going down but many of the allies performing even worse. For instance, the party now led by Nitish Kumar in Bihar, the JD(U), got just 8 seats, while Lalu's RJD got 24. The TDP went down to just 5 seats in Andhra Pradesh, where the Congress staged a revival and a young party with the name of Telangana Rashtra Samithi (TRS, which currently rules Telangana after the 2013 division of the state) also got 5 seats. Both the JD(U) and the TDP blamed the 2002 Gujarat riots as a factor for community mobilizations against them. In Bihar, videos and images of the riots were circulated by the RJD, and it damaged Nitish Kumar's standing. The two NDA allies that performed well were the BJD in Odisha and the SAD in Punjab—states where the 2002 Gujarat riots were not a factor, as the demographics did not include a significant Muslim population. The Trinamool Congress (TMC) was, at this point, an ally of the NDA and posted a miserable performance of just 1 seat in West Bengal.

Within the BJP, the Vajpayee camp also blamed the riots for the setbacks suffered by both the BJP and its allies in many parts of the country. The counter view in the BJP was that it was the lack of Hindutva issues that had robbed the party of its distinct identity and that it had to return to its core ideology to rebuild itself.

But the real story belonged to the Congress, which had staged a comeback after eight years out of power (two years of the United Front, followed by six years of the NDA).

A dramatic moment came when Sonia Gandhi 'sacrificed' the prime ministership and appointed economist Congressman and former RBI governor Manmohan Singh as prime minister. It was a wise decision. Public attention may have focused on the Congress but there were, again, many actors who enabled the existence of the UPA. After all, between them, the BJP and the Congress had just 283 seats, 11 above the simple majority mark of Parliament. The rest of the seats were held by other political parties, and India was again showing its federal nature.

A particularly spectacular result was posted from Tamil Nadu, where the Congress and a few smaller parties had joined the DMK-led front (the DMK had also supported the NDA, but changed tack again). This front won 35 seats in the state while the Left won 4—a complete rout for the AIADMK that had an understanding with the BJP. By now, the two major parties of the state, the DMK and the AIADMK, had settled into a fairly transactional relationship with whosoever came to power in Delhi. Coalitions were increasingly turning out to be about pragmatic arrangements and not ideological positions.

Anchored by the Left

Not so for the communists, however, who fought the Congress in a state such as Kerala but settled into backing the party when it deemed it a responsible act against a greater evil. A significant enabler of the UPA-1 was actually the bloc of left parties who chose to give outside support to the Manmohan Singh government. They had 61 seats in Parliament, from their bases in

West Bengal, Kerala and the single seat in Tripura. While other parties could be transactional in their relationship with the central government, be it BJP- or Congress-led, the Left was categorical in seeing the forces of Hindutva as the greater threat. The Left bloc, therefore, approached the project of propping up the UPA-1 with some ideological clarity. The UPA-1 also came up with certain pro-people schemes such as the Mahatma Gandhi National Rural Employment Guarantee Act (MGNREGA), which had the strong backing of the Left.

Having covered the UPA-1, I firmly believe that just as Vajpayee had become a moderating figure and an enabler of allies in 1998 and 1999, the influence of the Left kept the UPA-1 anchored in policies that were seen as pro-poor and pro-people. As it turned out, the Left was in decline in its biggest state, West Bengal, yet the ideological clarity they brought to the table in Delhi was a good influence on the UPA in its first term.

The other significant aspect of the 2004 result was the poor performance of both the BJP and the Congress—who fancied themselves national parties—in UP, the nation's largest state, which had 80 seats. This was the primary state that brought the BJP to national prominence, but the party picked up just 10 seats in 2004; their sole consolation was that the Congress had got just 9 from the home state of members of the Nehru-Gandhi dynasty, three of whom had been prime ministers.

At that time, the Congress was accused of being irrational in its approach to UP, and reams were written on its failure to come to a seat-sharing arrangement with the two principal parties of the state, namely the SP and the BSP. The SP posted a terrific result, winning 36 seats (the RLD got three, increasing the SP-RLD bloc to 39), while the BSP got 19. Neither joined the UPA government, but when required gave outside support. Such a moment came in July 2008, when the Left pulled out on the issue of the Indo-US nuclear deal, necessitating a trust vote that was passed with the help of the SP and the BSP.

By the time the 2009 election came around, the BJP was still crisis-ridden—the party was exploding with leadership clashes, ego tussles between the next generation of leaders after Vajpayee and Advani, and the lack of ideological clarity. The party did put together a lacklustre campaign around Advani, but it never really took off. The NDA performed miserably, and that was the time when obituaries of the BJP began to be written. Was the party over? Was Vajpayee a flash in the pan?

Politics Determined by Alliances

The BJP's seats had dropped from 138 to 116 and the NDA block posted 159 seats in all, leaving it with no chance of government formation. It's also interesting to see where vote shares stood in the election, as there would be a great change in 2014. From nearly 24 per cent of the votes in 2004, the BJP had now dropped to 18.9 per cent. The Congress had a 10 per cent lead, with 28.6 per cent of the national vote. This was a big change from the past decade. It is, therefore, educational to understand what was happening with vote shares in the preceding years.

In the 1996 election, the first where the BJP did better than the Congress, it won 161 seats, with 20.3 per cent of the votes. The Congress got fewer seats, just 141, but had an 8 per cent lead over the BJP, that is 28.8 per cent votes. Confusing, but what this means is that the Congress votes were scattered, while the BJP had concentrated support in certain seats/regions.

Both parties appeared head to head on their vote shares in 1998, but with the Congress just a nose ahead, with 25.8 per cent of the votes and the exact same number of seats as in 1996—141. The BJP vote share was 25.4, a few points behind the Congress, but the seats went up to 179.

What happened in the year that led to the 1999 election is also interesting. The BJP dropped its vote share to 23.7 per cent but won 182 seats. The Congress that year picked up on its vote share, which went up to 28.3 per cent, but dropped its seats to 114. The reason was simple: It was the arithmetic of the prepoll alliance that the BJP forged with smaller parties that saw the NDA surge ahead. We also get a sense of the changing politics from the increasing vote shares of the NDA allies in this period: 1996 (4 per cent), 1998 (10.8 per cent) and 1999 (11.3 per cent).

The point really was that in the era of the NDA and the UPA 1 and 2, politics was determined by alliance formation. In 2004, the BJP vote share dropped to 23 per cent, while that of the Congress went up to 26.4 per cent. What was remarkable about the 2009 verdict was that since the coalition era began, a government that completed a full term actually got elected again. What's more, the Congress tally went up. It got 205 seats, a gain of 60 from its 2004 tally of 145, and the vote share, too, went up to 28.6 per cent. The crash in the BJP's vote share, which dropped to 18.9 (below 20 per cent) in 2009, is, therefore, significant.

What also happened in 2009 was that the Congress actually won many seats at the cost of the left parties that had played an important role in propping up the UPA-1. First, one of those flip-flop journeys of coalition politics had happened with the TMC. Its leader, Mamata, had forged a prepoll arrangement with the Congress to take on the Left Front, with which the Manmohan Singh regime's relations had soured over the Indo-US nuclear deal. In West Bengal, the TMC got 19 seats and the Congress 7; the Left share shrank to 9, as it did in Kerala with the Congress-led front winning 16 of the state's 20 seats. From 61 seats in 2004, the Left bloc of MPs shrank to 20 seats from across India in 2009.

The other big achievement for the Congress was that it revived itself, somewhat, in UP, winning 21 of the state's 80 seats, while the BSP and the SP got 23 each. It was the SP that took a hit (it had 36 in 2004) when the Congress revived, again highlighting the common voter blocs that the Congress shared with parties that were potential allies in any anti-BJP front. Again the BSP and the SP did not join the government; the big allies in the regime were TMC, which had 19 seats, and the DMK, which had 18 (a small reversal from 2004 but still a substantial chunk). Sharad Pawar's Nationalist Congress Party (NCP), which by now was part of the alliance with the Congress in Maharashtra against the BJP-Shiv Sena alliance, had 9 seats. In conclusion, the UPA-2 was an alliance but with greater balance on the side of the Congress.

This meant that allies had lesser control over setting the narrative and tone for the regime. I believe this is at its heart what went wrong for UPA-2, so much so that by the end of its tenure, it was a deeply unpopular and discredited regime. UPA-1 had passed some empowering policies such as the Right to Information (RTI) and MGNREGA, the world's largest employment guarantee scheme. It seemed to have been a regime where caring for the poor seemed a priority, something that always worked for the Congress since Indira Gandhi silenced and checkmated her critics with the '*Garibi hatao*' slogan all those decades ago. Call it populism, but it works with the electorate in an overwhelmingly poor country.

Where the Congress Faltered

UPA-2 seemed to be a regime that turned rightwards on economic policy. Unshackled by the Left, it quickly tried to move policies that brought foreign direct investment (FDI) into new sectors. The TMC, for instance, pulled out of the government in 2012, demanding the reversal of the policy allowing FDI in retail. The regime also cracked down on NGOs and activists who opposed the handing over of lands to mining companies and the setting up of a nuclear facility in Tamil Nadu. Broadly, the regime seemed to prioritize pleasing international finance and big business. It did not have the human face that UPA-1 did. The biggest undoing of the regime was the perception that it was a corrupt government that went about pleasing capitalists and big businesses. Crony capitalism was now the biggest charge flung at the regime.

Within two years of performing so well, UPA-2 was tottering. If the TMC left in 2012, the DMK walked out in 2013 over the alleged involvement of its ministers in the 2G spectrum scandal. The DMK's alibi was the government's position on war crimes against Tamils in Sri Lanka at the United Nations Human Rights Council (UNHRC). But the government did not collapse because, once again, the BSP and the SP, along with smaller parties, gave outside support.

But a storm was brewing that would, temporarily, blow the Congress away.

Chapter 7

ANNA & AAP: THE TWILIGHT PHASE

A new movement that morphed into a political party did real damage to the UPA. And eventually, by 2014, the biggest beneficiary was the BJP and Modi. Here's what happened: By April 2011, large crowds had gathered in Delhi in what came to be known as the Anna movement. In other towns in India too, people gathered in protest and spoke of a great disenchantment with traditional politics and all-pervasive corruption in the system. The stated purpose of the India Against Corruption (IAC) group, the architect of the Anna movement, was to introduce a Jan Lokpal Bill, or an anti-corruption law. Arvind Kejriwal, RTI campaigner and activist, designed the movement. It was a lightning rod because it connected to a certain mood in the electorate as a spate of corruption charges rocked the UPA-2. In a country where large-scale farmer unrests or Dalit marches sometimes go unnoticed by the press, the media gave the Anna movement non-stop coverage, as it was the middle class that led the way, and its epicentre was in New Delhi. The RSS and yoga guru Baba Ramdev supplied the initial crowds until the movement gained momentum on its own.

Attending the gatherings, it seemed clear to me that the RSS had taken a tactical decision to back the movement and supply some of the manpower. God-men Baba Ramdev and Sri Sri Ravi Shankar were pivots of this movement. Post 2014, they would be close to the BJP establishment and the larger Sangh Parivar. One of the members of the IAC decision-making body was the decorated police officer Kiran Bedi, who would later join the BJP. At that time, however, no one claimed any political affiliation, saying they were there as part of a bigger public sentiment.

This movement would eventually gather enough force to knock the wind out of UPA-2. But it must also be stated that Kejriwal, after planning and executing the movement, would choose to tread a different path. He would establish a new party, the Aam Aadmi Party (AAP), in November 2012, with an ideology distinctly Left of Centre on economic policies and the promise that it would not, like the BJP, mine identity issues. The AAP would come to power in Delhi in February 2015 and would predominantly cater to the needs of the urban poor and the lower middle class.

But beyond Delhi, what Anna Hazare and the AAP did was create a huge disruption in national politics. First, the Anna movement that preceded the formation of the AAP led to a huge loss of face for the Congress, as day in and day out the party was being shamed for alleged corruption. The Congress seemed to be hollowed out and in danger of collapsing with just a push. Although the AAP would put down roots in Delhi, nationally the beneficiary would be the BJP when Modi, then Gujarat chief minister, would begin a powerful presidential-style campaign for 2014. First, the Modi-led BJP resoundingly beat the Congress in

2014, and then, six months later, in the Delhi assembly elections, the AAP demolished the Congress—it was a double whammy for the party, which was hit by both a conventional opponent, the BJP, and a newbie, the AAP.

In Delhi, a state it had ruled for three terms, the Congress got zero seats and its vote share crashed to 10 per cent. The BJP lost badly too, but its vote share still stood at 33 per cent. It was a loss of face for the BJP that had, just six months ago, won a historic mandate that had effectively ended the coalition era.

Chapter 8

THE ARITHMETIC OF THE MODI MAJORITY

The Anna movement and the Kejriwal-led AAP were disruptions, but the greatest disruption to the way politics was being managed in an era of coalitions was when Modi became prime minister in 2014. The NDA won 336 seats, of which 282 were won by the BJP. The Congress-led UPA won just 59 seats, of which 44 were won by the Congress, its lowest ever. It was such a pathetic performance that the party could not even become the official Opposition, as, to do so, a party had to get 10 per cent of the seats.

But the significant change was that after the 1984 election, this was the first time a party had crossed the majority mark on its own. Kudos to the Modi-led campaign, presidential in style and grandeur, but examine the vote share and the results more closely and you will see that it was the Opposition's failure to come to an understanding on seats, tactical or formal, which helped the BJP along the way. In the end, with just 31 per cent of the national vote, the BJP could manage the best conversion of votes to seats. As we have seen in earlier chapters, in the age of the Congress dominance, it, too, won disproportionate seats to its votes—but not on the scale that the BJP managed in 2014. The BJP had a 12 per cent increase in its vote share from 2009, but it could turn this into a 31 per cent increase in seats. This gave the appearance of dominance in the political space when, in fact, it was tenuous and disproportional.

The Congress vote share also dipped to an all-time low, at 19 per cent. But what is also significant about the 2014 result is that on the basis of vote shares, the BJP emerged as the dominant party in terms of seats, but the regionalization of the Indian electorate had not been stalled. Some parties, notably the BSP, got 20 per cent of the votes in UP but could not win a single seat. Broadly, this reinforced the principal of parties having to cross a certain threshold or coming to an understanding with another party to win seats. The BSP, for instance, had 4.1 per cent of the national vote share (in 2014) and small, loyal bases in many states, which is effective when the alliance parties dominate the narrative of those states. But in UP, the party faltered badly in 2014 by going it alone. The importance of being strong within a geographical location was also reinforced by the results from other states. The AIADMK, then led by Jayalalithaa, won 37 seats from Tamil Nadu, but its national vote share of 3.3 per cent was still less than that of the BSP, which won zero seats. Similarly, the TMC, led by Mamata, won 34 seats in West Bengal, although its national vote share was 3.8 per cent.

Yet, there was a 'national mood' in the popularity of one figure, Modi, which now helped the BJP capitalize on its national win and begin the conquest of multiple states. On 16 May 2014, the verdict was declared, and on 26 May Modi took the oath of office. The BJP then appeared to gain momentum in several states, where polls were held later that year.

In October 2014, the BJP defeated the Congress in Haryana and, in alliance with the Shiv Sena, wrested back Maharashtra from the Congress-NCP alliance. In December, the BJP managed to win in Jharkhand. The party also swept Jammu (again beating the Congress), while the People's Democratic Party (PDP) won in Kashmir, again leading to the formation of an unlikely coalition in J&K. (The PDP-BJP alliance would eventually fall under the weight of its ideological differences and even as the 2019 contest takes place, the sensitive border state is under President's rule).

In 2015, the BJP witnessed two significant electoral setbacks. First, the party faced a humiliating defeat against the AAP in Delhi, where PM Modi had positioned himself against Kejriwal. What that win indicated was that when a personality drives politics, another charismatic figure can be a formidable opponent. What followed later that year is more instructive for a work on coalition politics. In the assembly elections in Bihar, two opposing forces, both led by individuals who had been chief ministers (one of whom was in the chair), put together their differences to fight the BJP aside. The Grand Alliance, or the Mahagatbandhan, between Lalu's RJD and Nitish Kumar's JD(U) defeated the BJP. At that time, it was hailed as a model for the future, but we will examine later why the breaking of the alliance is also the sort of model that damages public faith in coalition politics.

In the Age of Modi and Shah

In 2016, the BJP won Assam, ruled for three terms by the Congress, and opened the gate to the Northeast. The same year, however, the TMC comfortably won a second term in West Bengal, confirming the trend seen in the Lok Sabha polls. Similarly, Jayalalithaa's AIADMK won Tamil Nadu with ease, while the Left Democratic Front (LDF) wrested Kerala from the Congress-led United Democratic Front (UDF). The left parties had incidentally been reduced to ten MPs in 2014, down from twenty in 2009 and sixty-one in 2004.

But 2017 brought the real windfall for the BJP, when it swept UP, confirming the trend established in 2014, when it had won 73 seats of the state's 80 (2 seats in this were won by a small ally called Apna Dal).

It also won Uttarakhand and was on such a muscular high that it managed to form coalition governments in Goa and Manipur in spite of the Congress having more seats (but short of a simple majority). The Congress, however, won in Punjab, which was essentially a vote against the BJP's long-term ally, the Akali Dal. Till the end of 2018, therefore, the BJP controlled governments in states that covered more than 60 per cent of the population.

But cracks were showing and alternative political strategies were being explored by the BJP's allies. In 2014, the two NDA allies with the largest number of MPs were the Shiv Sena, which won 18 seats, and the TDP, which had 16. The rest of the NDA allies did not cross into double digits. By March 2018, the TDP walked out of the NDA, partly due to the compulsions of state-level politics but also due to what they articulated as the arrogant and insensitive tone of the BJP leadership in Delhi. There were allegations that top BJP ministers did not give them the time of day.

Eventually, the TDP aligned with the Congress for state elections in Telangana—for which results were announced at the end of 2018—but was defeated by the TRS. But after the division of the state, the

TDP's main turf was Andhra Pradesh, where another state party, named the Yuvajana Sramika Rythu Congress Party, or the YSR Congress Party, was the challenger. It was led by Y.S. Jagan Mohan Reddy, the son of the late Congressman Y.S.R. Reddy, who had delivered the largest chunk of seats to the national party in the 2009 Lok Sabha election. (A small caveat to note is that undivided Andhra Pradesh had given the Congress 32 seats in 2009 and is now divided into two states, with three state parties at play: the TDP, which rules Andhra Pradesh, the YSR Congress Party, which the TDP sees as a challenger in the state, and the TRS, which is in power in Telangana and sees a threat in any potential revival of the Congress. What is interesting about this region is that Chandrababu of the TDP and K. Chandrasekhar Rao of the TRS, currently both chief ministers of their respective states, see themselves as big players in any coalition front that is put together. The TDP has some experience at this, while the TRS, a younger party, recognizes the sheer clout an independent front would bring to regional parties.)

In 2018, just a year before the general election, the NDA lost the TDP as an ally without finding an alternative partner. But what had also been happening is that the Shiv Sena had been routinely making statements against the BJP leadership, both at the Centre and in Maharashtra. This was the consequence of the state party feeling threatened by the clout of the national party, which was eating into its bases; again, they said the high command of the BJP did not consult them or give allies due respect. However, it is important to note that post the Pulwama attacks in Jammu and Kashmir, the BJP and the Shiv Sena have agreed on a seat-sharing pact for the Lok Sabha elections in Maharashtra this year. The BJP will contest 25 seats and the Shiv Sena 23 in the state. But whether this will help ease the distinct lack of trust between them remains to be seen.

A different scenario has unfolded for the NDA in Bihar. Nitish Kumar, who had parted ways with the NDA on the issue of Modi as PM in 2013 and had allied with Lalu in the 2015 assembly polls to defeat the BJP did an about-turn (against the mandate) in 2017. He went back to the arrangement of the BJP and the JD(U) sharing power in the state, but it's yet to be tested whether this arrangement can work in a Lok Sabha poll, as Lalu's party has always had a larger vote share in Bihar. Will a section of the electorate view Nitish Kumar's actions as a breach of trust?

Two smaller parties with caste-based votes that impact a few seats in Bihar have, however, left the NDA for the RJD-Congress alliance that will contest in 2019. What is also significant is that a veteran socialist, Sharad Yadav—former president of the JD(U), seven-term Lok Sabha member and two-term Rajya Sabha member, and an important figure in the NDA—parted ways with Nitish Kumar and is now throwing his weight behind any anti-NDA front.

Nitish Kumar is currently caught between a rock and a hard place. Chief Minister of Bihar since 2005, he thrived in the BJP of the Vajpayee era. But the BJP of that age gave great room and respect to allies, as it never imagined the party could get a simple majority on its own. Vajpayee was an amiable individual, lacking in ruthlessness, while Advani, the real strategist, believed in the process of incremental growth with the help of crutches in the form of allies in the states.

But the BJP in the age of PM Modi and Shah is vastly different. It tries to influence the mainstream media narrative and does not lean on allies but gradually takes over their space. Regional forces have therefore learnt to be wary of the new muscular BJP.

A case in point is the Janata Dal (Secular), or JD(S), in Karnataka, led by former prime minister Deve Gowda. When assembly elections took place in the Congress-ruled state in May 2018, the JD(S) got into a covert understanding with the BJP on some seats to curtail the power of the Congress. But when the results came in, the JD(S) did not help the BJP, which emerged as the single-largest party, to form the government. Instead, it formed a government with the Congress and got the chief minster's chair. It must be noted that the BJP moved heaven and earth to try to form a government in the state, but in spite of all its resources, it was thwarted.

The real shock for the BJP came at the end of 2018, when results to the assembly elections in Madhya Pradesh, Chhattisgarh and Rajasthan were announced. In one fell sweep, the BJP lost three state governments to the Congress, definitely a reality check for the party. The public narrative was again shifting. It seemed that the country was no longer going in the direction of greater dominance by the BJP. Now it is anyone's guess which party will lead the government that will come next.

Chapter 9

THE BUSINESS OF POLITICS

I have always believed that opaqueness in political funding is the reason Indian democracy at times seems to be hollowed out. Regardless of who is in power, huge swindles and scams unfold, because big political funders are often allowed to cheat the exchequer by elected representatives who should be guarding our money. But only some of the stories come out, and the Indian public has little information on the sources of the huge infusion of cash in our political system.

Money is very much part of any coalition arrangement. In the age of the UPA, for instance, the DMK was allegedly allotted 'financially lucrative' ministries such as communication and information technology; an alleged scam on the allocation of the 2G spectrum took place under the watch of the DMK's A. Raja, who was later arrested but eventually acquitted by the courts; and Dayanidhi Maran, another DMK minister, resigned as textile minister in 2011 over allegations that as telecom minister, he apparently arm-twisted the promoter of mobile service provider Aircel to sell out to Malaysian telecom firm Maxis Communications.

There is little to argue over the fact that large sums of money are eroding the Indian democracy, making regimes hostage to crony capitalists and middle-level operators. How did jeweller Nirav Modi and his uncle Mehul Choksi manage to defraud so many banks and flee the country? The public could have got some answers if we could have examined their accounts to check if either made donations to any political party. But most political parties, including the Congress and the BJP, are united in opposing the demand for greater transparency in political funding. Nobody with any clout in politics seems to want to regulate the deluge of money into politics. Simultaneously, data shows that MLAs and MPs become richer with every stint in power.

On the matter of creating coalitions, all those who cover politics know there is a 'rate' to get the support of independent MPs or a small party required to form a government in the event of a hung parliament or assembly. Very pragmatic arrangements are often made by independent MPs and regional parties to support a particular legislation as well. There has traditionally been a lot of quid pro quo in coalition politics, although the BJP, as alleged by the Opposition, has been attempting to break the financial back of parties that do not support it. It has been alleged by the Opposition that enforcement agencies are selectively used against those who do not support the government that came to power in 2014. All the current big players in the Opposition have said so: Priyanka Gandhi, Mamata Banerjee, Mayawati, Akhilesh Yadav, who are all facing inquiries by enforcement agencies.

On 8 November 2016, PM Modi made a dramatic address to the nation, announcing the demonetization of the ₹500 and ₹1,000 banknotes. The controversial step, he said, was designed to flush out black money and clog financial pipelines to terrorist organizations. However, since all the currency was returned to banks, critics say that the move did not help flush out black money. As for terrorism, in the Kashmir Valley, alienation has increased partly due to certain policies of the Modi regime. Demonetization has, therefore, not had any impact on the deteriorating situation in the Valley.

Besides slowing down the economy and crippling certain sectors, what demonetization did, however, was seriously inconvenience political parties that were in the habit of taking donations in cash, often in exchange for tickets. There are no clear figures, as such transactions operate in the black economy, but it is said that the cash entering the coffers of certain political parties was briefly hard to come by in the months following the demonetization announcement. There were particularly compelling reports of parties such as the BSP losing a lot of currency as they headed to an assembly poll in UP just a few months after demonetization.*

---

*'Election Commission lets BSP off in Rs 104 crore deposit post demonetisation', *Financial Express*, 12 May 2017, https://www.financialexpress.com/india-news/election-commission-lets-bsp-off-in-rs-104-crore-deposit-post-demonetisation/666106/

Simultaneously, Opposition parties have alleged that some BJP leaders and their friends had been alerted about demonetization and managed to change their notes before the announcement.*

At the point of writing this book, the BJP was the richest party in India's history.** This astounding increase in the party's wealth and the impoverishment of other parties really accelerated in the year after demonetization was announced, so it does trigger interesting speculation along intriguing lines of enquiry. But since the agencies are under government control, or on the mat in the Supreme Court, it is impossible to investigate the mystery of this soaring wealth. Unless there is a government change, this will remain one of the riddles of contemporary democracy.

There are, however, some facts that can be stated with authority, as they are based on income tax statements

---

*'BJP, its friends knew about demonetisation move: Opposition in RS', *The Hindu BusinessLine*, 15 January 2018, https://www.thehindubusinessline.com/news/national/bjp-its-friends-knew-about-demonetisation-move-opposition-in-rs/article9353277.ece

**Sunetra Choudhury, 'BJP Richest National Party, With Rs 1,034 Crore Declared Income: Report', NDTV, 11 April 2018, https://www.ndtv.com/india-news/bjp-richest-national-party-with-rs-1-034-crore-declared-income-report-1835718

that were submitted to the Election Commission of India (ECI). So this is not mere speculation about the costs of the BJP's heavily mounted and advertised campaigns, and rumours about unaccounted cash that circulate during election time. Let's just look at the figures that are available. In 2016–17, the ruling BJP's income soared to ₹1,034 crore from ₹570 crore in 2015–16, according to annual audit reports filed with the ECI on 8 February 2018. According to the audit report, the BJP's receipt for 2016–17 matched the receipts for *all* seven parties (including the BJP) listed as national parties in the previous year when the money came to ₹1,034 crore.

This report was carried as the lead story in the Delhi edition of *The Times of India* on 11 April 2018.*
This is an astounding figure, which means that in the year after demonetization, the BJP got two-third of the entire income of all national parties in India.

Still, it's not as if money alone determines outcomes. But in situations where mandates are not clear, financial heft can help a party come to power. All the same,

---

*Bharti Jain, 'BJP's income double that of other 6 national parties together', *The Times of India*, 11 April 2018, https://timesofindia. indiatimes.com/india/bjps-income-double-that-of-other-6-national-parties-together/articleshow/63704786.cms

while individual MPs can switch sides with abandon, larger regional parties have to be more cautious and also act in ways that do not annoy or alienate their voter blocs. For all the money in the world, therefore, the RJD, the SP and the TMC, for instance, cannot back the BJP today.

The BJP's wealth is way more than the Congress share during the UPA rule, in 2004–05 and 2013–14. When the UPA came to power in 2004, the Congress share touched 58 per cent of receipts given to national parties. But by 2013–14, the last year of the UPA-2, the Congress share was down to 39 per cent, while the BJP's jumped to 44 per cent.

The point this reinforces is that money moves in the direction of political power—and by 2013, big corporates were shifting donations from the Congress to the BJP. This also means that after the opening up of the Indian economy, a process that began in the late 1980s, no party has managed the domination of financial donations in the manner that the BJP has.

In 2014, according to figures filed with the ECI, the BJP spent ₹712 crore on the campaign. It was by far the most expensive campaign in the country's history. The irony was that after a decade in power, the Congress, mid-campaign, stopped sending funds to candidates in some parts of India who were expected to lose. Having ruled over the country for most of its history and presided over the opening up of the economy, the only explanation for the Congress being broke is that fund collection was carried out in such a haphazard and ad hoc manner that there was no real accountability. The BJP today, in the age of Modi and Shah, has a more centralized fund collection than during the Vajpayee era.

The conquest of new territories by the Modi-led BJP was well funded and expensively mounted on a grand scale. It is worth repeating that although the BJP did not win any election in Goa or some smaller states in the Northeast, it had enough clout, political and financial, to manage government formation with the help of smaller parties.

Recent elections in the US show that 91 per cent of the candidates who spent more won.* In the last Lok Sabha elections in India, the richest candidate

---

*Tess VandenDolder, 'Political candidates with the most money almost always win their election', DC Inno, 7 April 2014, https://www.americaninno.com/dc/political-candidates-with-more-money-win-elections-study-inforgraphic/

won 84 per cent of the time, with the poorest of all candidates losing their deposit on every seat.* In both the world's largest and the world's most powerful democracy, therefore, money is a big factor marking the difference between victory and defeat. US President Donald Trump is a billionaire who threw his money into a campaign, which he pulled off. The BJP has steadily become the richest party in India's history under the leadership of Modi and Shah. Yet, in December 2018, the party lost states where it ruled. One of the reasons the Congress could fight the astounding wealth, cadre strength and manpower of the BJP in Madhya Pradesh and Chhattisgarh was that it posited wealthy individuals as leaders. And since the party per se was broke, its state leaders raised the money or put their own into the campaign. There was also some amount of 'round-tripping' in the process, whereby the state leaders and candidates actually raised the money and it headed back to Delhi and was returned to the state. The

---

*Neelanjan Sircar, 'Money matters in Indian elections: Why parties depend on wealthy candidates', *Hindustan Times*, 26 July 2018, https://www.hindustantimes.com/india-news/money-matters-in-indian-elections-why-parties-depend-on-wealthy-candidates/story-z81zpqywH7yA1rx3dLzVrN.html

process is complicated and difficult to comprehend—and stories about political finance are difficult to prove.

The BJP is today a rich party, while the Congress is a poor one with some very rich leaders, some of whom recently came to power in elections where three BJP chief ministers were defeated. There are regional parties, too, that have astounding wealth and make a display of it. Being in power is what gives a political party financial clout. This means that candidates spend huge sums because they believe they will recover the money if they win. Money does impact politics, and any coalition that is formed in the future will also be looking to profit from the business of being in politics.

Chapter 10

UTTAR PRADESH: THE COALITION CONUNDRUM

Arithmetic dictates that if all the regional parties of India got together, no national party could survive very long. This is, however, not a possibility, as, in some important states, regional parties are competing more fiercely with one another than with the national parties. Take the DMK versus the AIADMK, or the TDP versus the YSR Congress Party/TRS, both in the south of India.

In each of the two large Hindi heartland states of UP and Bihar, there are two significant parties that operate (besides the national parties). In UP, it is the SP and the BSP, and in Bihar, it is the RJD and the JD(U). As the short-lived but arithmetically significant Grand Alliance or Mahagatbandhan in Bihar indicated, a combination of two region-specific parties can be devastating for a national player.

UP is an even more complex state, with certain peculiarities. First, it is the country's most populous state. Second, it is a state where the upper castes are numerically strong, constituting nearly 20 per cent of the population (it is home to the largest numbers of Brahmins in the country, who make up 10 per cent of the state's population). Third, the three contested sites where the VHP, the BJP and the RSS claim that mosques were built after destroying temples are in Kashi, Mathura and Ayodhya, all located in UP. Fourth, it is the home state of the Nehru-Gandhi dynasty and of most of India's prime ministers. And fifth, it is the state that has witnessed both backward caste and Dalit mobilization on political lines.

Let us briefly delve into UP's political history to get an insight into what the future can hold. First, we will learn that it has been the theatre of every coalition experiment that has happened in the country since the erosion of the Congress domination. The process began in the 1967 state election. The Congress got just 199 seats, short of a majority in the 425-seat assembly (since the creation of Uttarakhand, the assembly strength is 403). The Jana Sangh made its presence felt with 98 seats, indicating that the Hindutva sentiment was of an old vintage in the state.

Revolving-Door Politics

The first actor of the UP coalition drama has to be Charan Singh, the Jat leader who broke from the Congress to form the Bharatiya Kranti Dal (BKD). He was backed by socialists such as Lohia, who had already come up with the doctrine of anti-Congressism, and by Jana Sangh leader Nanaji Deshmukh. In April 1967, Charan Singh was sworn in as chief minister of the state at the head of the Samyukta Vidhayak Dal (SVD), a coalition ranging from CPI(M) on the Left to the Jana Sangh on the Right, and small parties such as the Republican Party of India, the Swatantra Party and a clutch of independents.

What followed over the next four years was classic coalition instability, which saw four chief ministers in and out of the revolving door. Each constituent of the coalition had its own agenda and kept pushing it. In less than a year, Charan Singh resigned, and a year of President's rule followed. Elections were held in 1969, and Charan Singh's party—which had significantly begun to represent a section of the middle and rich peasantry, including Muslims of western UP—won 98 seats, while the Jana Sangh share dropped to 49. The Congress won 211 and managed a chief minister, but the party split in a year. Charan Singh returned as chief minister, this time supported by the Congress faction loyal to Indira Gandhi. More drama followed and President's rule was again imposed. After another election that failed to give a clear verdict, another patchwork socialist regime was propped up, which lasted five months.

Brahmin Party?

What is instructive is that the Congress of that era only turned to Brahmins for leadership positions. Congressman Kamalapati Tripathi, one of the Brahmin doyens of the party, became chief minister for two years, from 1971 to 1973, and when his government fell due to a revolt by the police, another Brahmin from Garhwal, Hemwati Nandan Bahuguna, became chief minister in November 1973. He lasted until 1975 but then was pushed out due to differences with Indira Gandhi's son, Sanjay Gandhi. A third Brahmin, this time from Kumaun, Narayan Dutt (N.D.) Tiwari, became chief minister, at the time that Indira Gandhi imposed the Emergency on the country.

When the Janata Party won the Lok Sabha elections in 1977, the Tiwari government was sacked and, in the elections that followed, the Janata Party won 352 of the 425 seats. But what was happening at the Centre during the Janata years was being replicated in the state with faction fights and ego tussles over the chief minister's post. Chandra Shekhar pitched for a Dalit chief minister, while the Charan Singh faction, along with socialist leader Madhu Limaye, backed a Yadav. Eventually, Ram Naresh Yadav, an MP from Azamgarh, became chief minister from 1977 to 1979, and the Jana Sangh was part of the government. Kalyan Singh (who would later become the BJP's chief minister in the state) was health minister, while Mulayam (who would go on to have three terms as the state's chief minister) was then the minister in charge of cooperatives. However, Ram Naresh Yadav, too, resigned due to a case of police atrocities, and there was briefly another chief minister in charge, until Indira Gandhi returned to power and dismissed the Janata government.

The Congress swept the 1980 election, back to primacy with 309 of the 425 seats in UP. Now, besides Brahmins, it also began elevating another forward caste, the Thakurs—and V.P. Singh, the king of a small principality, became chief minister. What is fascinating about that age is that V.P. Singh's tenure saw a lot of violence amid charges of fake police encounters. In 1981, the Behmai massacre took place, in which twenty Rajputs were killed by the bandit Phoolan Devi. Dacoits eventually killed V.P. Singh's elder brother Justice Chandra Shekhar Pratap Singh, following which V.P. Singh resigned. In 1982, another Brahmin, Shripati Mishra, ruled for two years until 1984, when N.D. Tiwari was brought back for another tenure as chief minister. He was in the chair when Indira Gandhi was assassinated, after which the Congress swept UP again. Rajiv Gandhi, in 1985, replaced him with Vir Bahadur Singh, a Thakur leader from Gorakhpur (the same place from where current UP Chief Minister Yogi Adityanath, also a Thakur, heads a religious order). Vir Bahadur Singh got nearly three years but was replaced by N.D. Tiwari, under whom the Congress was defeated in 1989.

Since then, the Congress has never formed a government in the state. But what must be noted is that since 1967, resistance to the party has been visible, although scattered into various ideological streams. But the point is that the electorally crucial state has never been a cakewalk for the Congress. The Jana Sangh, the socialists and the peasant forces have all been active in UP for half a century. In hindsight, we can also say that some of the Congress's atrophy can be linked to the fact that in the matter of leadership, the party never showed the capacity to look beyond Brahmins and Thakurs. In eight years, from 1980 to 1988, the Congress national leadership changed UP chief ministers six times, choosing only between the two forward castes. This would matter when 'Mandal and mandir' would explode on to the UP stage.

As we have seen, V.P. Singh eventually left the Congress and became prime minister when the Janata Dal came to power, with support from the BJP. Assembly elections followed in UP, and Mulayam formed the government—a replication of what was happening at the Centre. But after Lalu stopped Advani's Ram temple rath yatra and arrested him, the BJP withdrew support from both the Centre and the UP government. V.P. Singh resigned, and the Congress backed Chandra Shekhar; Mulayam survived a bit longer, as he backed the Chandra Shekhar faction.

Period of Chaos

The Centre and the state, which, until recently, had regimes that were given outside support by the BJP, were now at the mercy of the Congress. The entire exercise was precarious and the Congress soon withdrew support. Both governments fell once the inevitable happened, but Mulayam went on to establish himself as a long-distance player in UP politics.

'Mandal and mandir' was now furiously playing out in the state. The BJP was also quick to propel OBC leaders forward, such as Kalyan Singh in UP and Uma Bharti in Madhya Pradesh. Both were OBC leaders of the Lodh caste and deeply committed to the Ram temple movement—so, in a sense, they were a combination of both Mandal and mandir.

In the 1991 assembly election, the BJP, led by Kalyan Singh, won 221 seats in the 425-member house. But once the Babri mosque was demolished in December 1992, Kalyan Singh was sacked, along with other BJP chief ministers—Sunder Lal Patwa of Madhya Pradesh, Bhairon Singh Shekhawat of Rajasthan and Shanta Kumar of Himachal Pradesh.

What followed next is what is to be attempted in the future. Mulayam, who had founded the SP in 1992, approached the BSP for a strategic understanding. The BSP was the other big party that had emerged in UP in the Mandal era, but one that drew on the power of the Dalits. The founder of the BSP, Kanshi Ram, was arguably a political genius who understood that the Dalits could be mobilized as a distinct voter bloc. His protégé, Mayawati, was a tough no-nonsense practitioner of the craft of maximizing clout by speaking against the upper castes and empowering those at the bottom of the caste pyramid. The party would develop a very transferable and loyal voter bloc, for whom they achieved empowerment that was radical and transformative in its scale at that time. Because the BSP also developed the most transferable vote bank in north India, they could get into arrangements with different political parties to maximize their own influence.

In 1992, the SP and the BSP agreed to not contest against each other in the assembly polls. The SP contested 256 seats and won 109; the BSP contested 164 seats and won 67. Mulayam was chief minister, but in 1995, Mayawati walked out, reducing the government to a minority. This led to what is known as the 'guest house incident', in which Mayawati and BSP legislators claimed they were attacked by SP henchmen—Mayawati even said she could have been killed. This incident snapped the possibility of an arrangement between the two parties—until now, more than 25 years later.

The result was that the BJP decided to play Mayawati's saviour. There was great symbolism in the BJP stepping up: They could subsequently claim to have played a historic role in enabling a Dalit woman to become chief minster of the country's most populous state. Perhaps this enhanced the BJP's standing, and in the 1996 assembly election, the BJP got 174 seats, 39 short of majority. The assembly was kept in suspended animation, following which President's rule was imposed.

Then the BJP entered into an arrangement with the BSP, which had sixty-seven MLAs. The understanding was that each party would have a chief minister for six months each by rotation. Mayawati got her first six months but when it was Kalyan Singh's turn, she alleged that he had revoked orders issued by her that benefited Dalits, and withdrew support.

By now Mayawati had ended the arrangement with Mulayam and ditched the BJP. Desperate, the BJP resorted to breaking other parties with the help of the speaker of the assembly. A new group called Janatantrik BSP was created, as was another called the Akhil Bharatiya Loktantrik Congress, which lent support to the BJP government headed by Kalyan Singh. The Congress-appointed governor dismissed Kalyan Singh's government and swore in Jagdambika Pal of the Congress. Kalyan Singh challenged his dismissal in the Allahabad High Court and was sworn in again as chief minister until 1999. But this was essentially a period of chaos and a shakedown of the old order.

Still, the BJP had begun a period of electoral decline and the number of seats in the Lok Sabha from the state and in the assembly began to drop. Outstepped by rivals, Kalyan Singh, too, left the party for a while and, in 2000, Rajnath Singh, a Thakur, was made chief minister by the BJP. But in the 2002 election, the BJP lost, getting just 88 seats in the state. What is worth noting about the BJP's first stints with power in the state is that the party was on the ascendant in the years following the Ram temple agitation. But in the period that the BJP led a government at the Centre—from 1998 to 2004—the party was in decline in the largest state. This was a curious dichotomy in the ebb and rise of the BJP.

Another hung assembly delivered by the electorate of the state in 2002 again saw President's rule, followed by Mayawati's third coming as chief minister (this time for two months). The BSP and the BJP dissidents now propped up Mulayam, whose SP had emerged as the single-largest party with 143 seats (the BJP had 88 and the BSP 98, hence they had attempted to come together to ward off Mulayam).

What is also worth taking note of is that the Congress tally in 2002 was down to 25. Eventually, Mulayam managed to run a minority government for nearly four years. It was also during this period that the SP got its largest chunk of thirty-six MPs in the Lok Sabha after the 2004 election.

End of Coalitions

And then suddenly in 2007, the era of coalitions in UP came to an end. The BSP won a simple majority with 206 of the state's 403 seats (Uttarakhand had been created in 2000, so the size of the assembly was a bit smaller). Mayawati pulled this off by also reaching out to the Brahmins, but not the Thakurs, who also symbolize muscle power in the state. By the time her term ended in 2012, she had managed quite a feat. Since 1960, she became the first chief minister in UP to complete five years in office.

The next verdict was also decisive. In 2012, Mulayam's 38-year-old son led the SP to victory, winning 224 of the 403 seats. Akhilesh Yadav would develop a profile as a young, dynamic leader with a good head on his shoulders. He, too, had a full term in office. But by the time his term ended, the Modi wave had changed the political demographics of India. In the 2014 Lok Sabha polls, the BJP swept 73 of the state's 80 seats. When the assembly polls took place just under three years later, in 2017, the BJP won a three-fourth majority, getting 312 seats. The SP was reduced to 47 and the BSP to 19, while the Congress had

7. Although the election was fought in Modi's name, the BJP placed as chief minister Adityanath, the head priest of a religious order in Gorakhpur and a hardline Hindu figure.

Forging a Workable Coalition

What the BJP's huge 2017 victory in UP did was drive the SP and the BSP together again. They began contesting by-elections with each other's support. In March 2018, just a year after the SP had been demolished by the BJP in the state, the SP put up candidates in the Lok Sabha by-elections in Phulpur and Gorakhpur, the latter being the current chief minister's constituency. The BSP did not contest, but told its supporters to back the SP. The mighty BJP was defeated and Adityanath humiliated. Two months later, another by-election took place for the Kairana seat in western UP. This time it was contested by the RLD (the party now run by Charan Singh's descendants). The SP gave huge logistical support while the BSP did not oppose the candidature. The BJP put everything into fighting the poll, but was again defeated.

The three by-elections of 2018 reveal that the only

way to defeat the BJP in UP is to manage the index of Opposition unity. Joint campaigns and a strategic division of seats is the sensible way forward for the Opposition parties in the state. They should ideally put their traditional rivalry (even enmity) aside, and hang together or sink together. The extent to which they can manage this or fail at this is arguably the biggest factor that will determine the outcome of the 2019 general election. The formula for success for those who oppose the BJP, therefore, lies in their ability to forge a workable coalition.

Epilogue

THE NUMBERS LABYRINTH

The most perplexing thing about analysing coalitions is that until we get the exact numbers from an election, we cannot predict any formula. What we can do, however, is a quick scan of the country to examine which parties prevail in which state and what arrangements they can be persuaded or compelled into having. This is a speculative exercise but one worth engaging in, albeit with cautionary words that we are only examining possibilities.

First, let us conclude our speculation about UP and Bihar, the Indo-Gangetic plains that the BJP swept in 2014. We have already seen that an SP-BSP alliance is a lethal combination for the BJP. Yet, there is confusion about whether the Congress, which has shown signs of a revival in the recent assembly polls, can be accommodated in a grand alliance or whether it will be going it alone. After all, the arithmetic shows that the greater the index of Opposition unity, the greater the damage to the BJP in UP.

As things stand in early February 2019, the Congress is likely to fight alone, and it's not clear whether this will help or hurt the BJP. There are too many unknown elements in UP this time. Two traditional foes, the SP and the BSP, are fighting together; Priyanka Gandhi will step out of the family seats of Amethi and Rae Bareli and campaign in more seats; and it is still unclear whether the hardline positions of Adityanath, a controversial figure, are hurting or helping his party. Is the ideology being calibrated in a sensible manner? Is the harping on the Ram mandir issue a reminder of the BJP's failure to build a temple or a symbol of determination to continue to try and build one? Could ennui be setting in among voters when they hear the

Ram incantation? Will the notion of a muscular Hindu identity post Pulwama generate passions even as the Ram mandir issue fails to?

There are challenges confronting the opposing side as well. The inbuilt tension earlier examined in this book is again on display—the Congress and the regional parties of UP in many instances have the same voter blocs that they compete for. Regional parties would like the Congress to be a junior partner, yet the Congress may imagine it can repeat a performance such as that of 2009, when it got 21 seats on its own from the state. That year the Congress had sought an alliance with the Mulayam-led SP and been rebuffed.

UP's peculiar social demographics, which has a 20 per cent upper-caste vote (10 per cent of which is Brahmins), also contribute to the Congress's hopes. As we have seen, when it was a player in the state, the Congress overwhelmingly patronized Brahmins, with a few Thakurs also getting a turn at power. There is a theory being put out that the Congress can work in concert with the SP-BSP alliance and damage the BJP in seats where it would attract the Brahmin votes. The subplot to this theory is the reality that within UP, Adityanath is not just seen as a hardline Hindutva figure, but also as a Thakur. He is accused by Brahmins and other castes of promoting what is referred to as 'Thakurvaad'. Perceptions of caste resentment are indeed a factor of politics in the state, and it's difficult to determine the extent of the damage that the BJP will suffer. The situation in UP is, therefore, not clear at the time of writing this book.

Bihar (40 seats) has now settled into a fairly straightforward contest, with the RJD leading the Opposition ranks and the Congress part of the alliance, along with a few caste-based small parties. This front will take on the JD(U)-BJP alliance. There is less confusion about the Bihar contest, as the two regional parties are on opposing sides, unlike the BSP and the SP, which have been forced by circumstance to try and fight together. Still, nothing is sealed in politics, until it is formally announced. The Bihar battle is also interesting in that the BJP has decided to cede more seats to the JD(S) and fight for a fewer number of seats than it won in 2014. Somewhat late in the day, with the 2019 battle looming, the Modi-Shah-led BJP has begun the process of trying to show more humility to allies.

The other big state is Maharashtra (48 seats) and the

conventional arrangement is the BJP-Shiv Sena versus the Congress-NCP. That is what has finally happened: After attacking the BJP for the past few years, the Shiv Sena has agreed to a seat-sharing arrangement with it. A few months down the line, by October 2019, the state is scheduled to have assembly elections as well and there is a possibility of the assembly polls being advanced to take place with the national elections. The Shiv Sena has bigger stakes in the assembly elections and resents being pushed to being junior partner in the state. It has no doubt been exploring covert arrangements to cut the BJP to size, but there are limits to such an exercise. Ultimately, the Shiv Sena had no option but to align with the BJP. The question that now arises with regard to the BJP-Shiv Sena arrangement in Maharashtra is how do workers on the ground suddenly coordinate when the Shiv Sena has launched so many verbal and political attacks on the BJP post 2014? The two parties do, however, share an ideological orientation.

In the three Hindi heartland states where assembly elections took place recently—Madhya Pradesh (29 seats), Rajasthan (25 seats) and Chhattisgarh (11 seats)—the BJP had virtually swept all seats in 2014, but the tally is certain to come down.

The Congress is likely to perform better in the Lok Sabha as it continues to leverage the growing agricultural crisis and failure to create jobs by the Modi government. But every step of the way, the BJP, with its committed cadres, will fight back. In Gujarat (26 seats) too, it's a direct BJP-versus-Congress contest, and, again, because it had swept the state, there is no scope for the BJP to do better.

The elections to the state assemblies of Odisha (21 seats) and Andhra Pradesh (25 seats) will take place along with the Lok Sabha polls. The dominant party in Odisha, the BJD, will serve its own interests, with no strong ideological position on which front it will support at the Centre. Similarly, in Andhra Pradesh, the assembly polls will take place simultaneously. The contest is primarily between the TDP and the YSR Congress Party. Currently, the TDP is a Congress ally, but again, depending on the arithmetic, either party can go with either front.

The state of Tamil Nadu (39 seats) has witnessed some dramatic changes, with the AIADMK splintering into various factions after Jayalalithaa's death. One of the factions that currently rule the state has now entered into an alliance with the BJP. Cine stars, too, have entered the fray, but the expectation is that a traditional party, the DMK (which, too, lost an iconic father figure with the demise of K. Karunanidhi), will dominate politics in the Lok Sabha polls. And the DMK is currently quite firmly with the UPA, so much so that its leader, M.K. Stalin, recently demanded that Rahul Gandhi be declared the prime ministerial candidate of the UPA, causing consternation among other regional parties. What this also indicates is that in the south of India, Rahul Gandhi is an asset to any alliance and carries the family charisma. The northern parts of the country have proven a greater challenge for him, but a breakthrough could happen. Still, as far as Tamil Nadu parties go, it is good to remember that parties from the state have in the past chosen to have pragmatic relationships with whosoever comes to power in Delhi.

In Kerala (20 seats), the traditional fight is between the Congress and the Left-led fronts. The BJP is always hopeful of getting a seat here, but either way, most MPs from this state cannot back the NDA. In the south, the BJP's best chances lie in picking up seats in Karnataka (28), but here, too, it is going to confront some strong arithmetic, as the JD(S) and the Congress, which rule the state in an alliance, have declared that they will also be contesting the parliamentary elections after a pre-election division of seats.

A complex situation is developing in West Bengal (42 seats). The TMC, a powerful force, is in office, but the presence of the BJP is growing in the state and the party claims it will pick up a few seats. The problem lies in assessing what kind of arrangement the Congress will get into. The left parties would like the Congress to support them in an alliance against Mamata. As both are fairly reduced forces in the state, it's unclear whether they will be helping themselves or the BJP when such an alliance is actually made. The best option for the Congress would be an alliance with the TMC. It would also be sensible for the Congress to not get on the wrong side of the West Bengal Chief Minister in the event of an alliance formation in future. The Left, whatever their parliamentary strength, will back the UPA. Mamata, whose supporters say they see her as the PM, will negotiate hard in the event of the NDA being defeated in 2019.

In reality, it is unlikely that Mamata would want to shift to the Centre, as there is no second-rung leadership in her party in volatile West Bengal. Such positioning about possible PM candidates is, however, useful as rallying points for loyalists during campaigns and bargaining chips subsequently. It also invokes a certain sub-nationalist sentiment that Mamata has been using to fight off the BJP's attempts to create bases along the Hindu-Muslim fault line in her state. What she would want, however, is to have a big say in who becomes the leader of the UPA.

In J&K, which is now under President's rule, the BJP has wrested the Jammu region from the Congress, but certain reverses are inevitable in the state that has just 6 seats. Either the PDP or the National Conference (NC) will win from the Kashmir Valley, although hardly any votes are likely to be cast after the post-Pulwama crackdown in Kashmir. In states such as Haryana (10 seats), Uttarakhand (5 seats) and Himachal Pradesh (4 seats), the fights are direct between the BJP and the Congress, with a regional party also in play in Haryana. The BJP had done very well in 2014 in these states and there is limited scope for growth. Punjab (13 seats) is currently held by the Congress; it will be the NDA partner Akali Dal that will be seeking to wrest some seats.

The same logic applies to Delhi, which has 7 seats, all currently held by the BJP. Unless the AAP, which rules the state, manages to come to an understanding with the Congress, which is recovering some of its vote shares in the city-state, it is a splintered vote we are looking at. But in the national capital, the AAP is certainly a bigger force than the Congress, which would have to agree to play junior partner. Can the Congress stoop to conquer?

The outcome in many states will also depend on whether people want to vote for Modi during a national election and differently during a state poll. There are way too many imponderables in the picture. The BJP says it expects gains in the Northeast, but how many seats does that add up to? Assam has 14 and all the other Northeastern states combined have 10 Parliament seats. Even if the BJP sweeps the Northeast (which is unlikely), it will be in trouble if it loses ground in UP and the Hindi heartland.

Possible Coalition Formations

We are on the cusp of events that we cannot fully foresee. The questions that linger are these: Is Rahul Gandhi going to revive the Congress after being dismissed as a lightweight—as both his mother, Sonia

Gandhi, and grandmother, Indira Gandhi, were? Is Priyanka Gandhi really going to change the chemistry of the campaign? Will PM Modi have another big formula for 2019 to revive interest in his campaign? Will there be a big disruption regarding our relations with Pakistan that will impact elections in ways that we cannot foresee?

Are there dark horses in the race, such as the BJP's Nitin Gadkari, who will be put forward in the event of a defeat for the Modi-led BJP, so that another federal front can be an option, such as that run by Vajpayee? Is Mayawati's prime ministerial ambition real? There is a certain symbolism in a Dalit woman making it to the top job. But there is also a counter polarization in the face of strong figures taking over a coalition. A nonentity who offends and threatens no one sometimes works better for a coalition than a strong leader of one particular party of a specific region.

Dramatic events undoubtedly impact perceptions and voter choice. As we have seen, the terror strike in Pulwama has already changed the backdrop of the 2019 elections. War politics is also politics in a nation that has a working electoral democracy. The BJP says that only a strong leader such as Modi can lead successful action against a perceived enemy nation; the Opposition says the security situation in the Valley has only worsened under the BJP watch. Certainly, we cannot ignore the fact that a war-like situation would impact politics.

But in the end, it will all be about numbers. As we tumble down on the roller coaster of possible coalition formations, we shall not know until the last vote has been counted. But what we do know is this: Prepoll arrangements make more durable coalitions that last their terms. There has been some talk of the Opposition working on a CMP, but nothing definitive has emerged so far.

A shaky government, beset with ego battles, also collapses quickly, giving another occasion to the dominant national party of the age to stage a comeback. A neutral but respected figure, such as Manmohan Singh, could pull off a plausible coalition for one of his two terms. A likeable and charismatic figure such as Vajpayee could do it too. PM Modi is the kind of individual who can pull off anything he sets his mind to, but during his twelve years in Gujarat and his one term in Delhi, he never had to rule by consensus.

Will he have to do so in future, or will there be dramatic changes in 2019? Only a fool would say they know what is coming. The Indian public has a way of throwing curve balls and surprising those who presume to know. The Indian electorate will let us know in the summer of 2019 when temperatures are at their highest. Both metaphorically and literally, we shall have a hot Indian political summer.

INDEX

Aam Aadmi Party (AAP), 76–79, 80, 83, 123–24
'Absolute' Leadership, 9–14
Adityanath, Yogi, 106, 113, 116–17
Advani, Lal Krishna, 41, 53–54, 69, 88
    creator of the new vibrant BJP, 54
    See also Ram temple agitation
Agitational identity politics, 42. *See also* Hindutva
Agricultural crisis, 120
Akhil Bharatiya Loktantrik Congress, 110
All India Anna Dravida Munnetra Kazhagam (AIADMK), 46, 57, 67, 82, 84, 100, 120

Alternative political strategies, 85
Ambani, Dhirubhai, tax raids, 36
Anna movement, 76–79
Anti-BJP-ism, 23, 47
Anti-Congress forces, coalition of, 23
Anti-Congressism, 22–27
Anti-Hindi agitation, 23
Apna Dal, 84
Article 370, abolition of, 60
Asom Gana Parishad (AGP), 37, 39, 63

Babri mosque, 41, 46, 53, 108. *See also* Ram mandir agitation
Bachchan, Amitabh, tax raids on, 36
Bahujan Samaj Party (BSP), 10, 15–16, 20, 40, 43, 69, 72–73, 75, 82–93, 101, 108–13, 116, 118
Ballot box, 20
Banerjee, Mamata, 55, 62, 72, 82, 92, 122–23
Bangladesh, formation of, 29
Bangladeshi refugees, 29
Barnala, Surjit Singh, 55
Bedi, Kiran, 77
Bharatiya Jana Sangh, 25
Bharatiya Janata Party (BJP), 2, 8–9, 11–12, 15–17, 20, 25, 29–30, 35, 37–38, 40–42, 44–48, 50–71, 73, 76–85, 87–89, 91–92, 94–99, 101, 106–26

agitational politics, 41
alliance against the, 17
crash in the vote share, 72
electoral setbacks, 83
electoral strength of, 61
farmers' welfare, 12
hardline position, 59
income, 95
national prominence, 69
poor performance, 68
pre-election alliance, 58, 61
Ram mandir issue, 41, 46, 116–17
richest party in India, 94, 98
rise of, 56, 111
setbacks in state elections, 11 66, 83
-Shiv Sena alliance, 73, 87, 119
shock for, 89
simple majority, 2, 8–9, 20, 44
spending on campaign, 96
strong base in states, 16
Vajpayee era, 54–63
victory in UP, 113
vote share, 8, 20, 71–72, 81
windfall for, 84
Bharatiya Kranti Dal (BKD), 102
Bharti, Uma, 107
Biju Janata Dal (BJD), 39, 65, 120
Black economy, 93
Bofors scandal, 36. *See also* Gandhi, Rajiv
Brahmin Party, 103–7

Caste-based parties, 42
Caste-based votes, 88

Chaudhary, Jayant, 42
Chautala, Om Prakash, 39
Choksi, Mehul, 91
Civil liberties, 31
'Coalesce', 2
Coalition era, 71, 79
Coalition of anti-Congress forces, 25
Coalition of political forces, 32
Coalition of states, 3
Coalition rule, 2, 9
Coalitions and consensus, cardinal principles of, 10
Common Minimum Programme (CMP), 52, 60, 126
Communist Party of India (CPI), 20, 25, 48, 102
Communist Party of India (Marxist) CPI(M), 48
Congress (O), 25–26, 30
Congress, 8, 11–12, 14–27, 29–38, 40–43, 45–50, 52, 55, 61, 64–75, 78–81, 83–86, 89, 91, 96–99, 102–3, 105–7, 110–12, 116–24
  achievement for, 72
  devastation of, 10
  dominance of, 26
  in early Independent India, 21
  grip on absolute power, 22
  issue of succession, 21–22
  minimum income for poor, 12
  -NCP alliance, 83
  party under 'supreme

leader', 29
poor party with rich leader, 99
poor performance of, 68
Priyanka Gandhi's entry, 15–16
sign of revival, 14, 65, 85–86, 116
split of, 25, 103
vote share, 20, 70–72, 79, 81, 124
vote share, 81
zero seats in Delhi, 79
Crony Capitalism, 74

Dalits, 108, 110
Democratic coalition of interests, 29
Demonetization, 92–95
Desai, Morarji, 6, 22, 30, 32, 42
Deshmukh, Nanaji, 102
Deve Gowda H.D., 6, 48, 50, 89
'Dharma' of coalition politics, 60
Domination of financial donations, 96
Dravida Munnetra Kazhagam (DMK), 23, 37, 49, 67, 73–74, 91, 100, 121
vs. AIADMK, 100
Dynastic politics, 49

Economic growth, 4, 6–7
Ego tussles, 69, 104
Election Commission of India (ECI), 93, 95–96
Electoral decline, period of, 110
Electoral democracy, 20, 31, 125
Electoral processes, 5
Emergency, 31–32,

52, 104. *See also* Gandhi, Indira
English-speaking elite. *See* Nehru Jawaharlal
Erdoğan, Recep Tayyip, 13–14

Farmers' welfare, 12
Fernandes, George, 30, 55, 58, 61–62
Feudals and former princes, 24
Financial donations, domination of, 96
'Financially lucrative' ministries, 91
First general election (1952), 20
First-past-the-post system, 8, 20
Flip-flop journeys of coalition, 72
Foreign direct investment (FDI), 74

'Foreigner'. *See* Gandhi, Sonia

Gadkari, Nitin, 125
Gandhi, Indira, 2, 6, 15, 22–23, 25–26, 28–32, 34–35, 45, 73, 103–5, 125
  assassination, 35, 45, 105
  emergency imposition by, 31, 104
Gandhi, Mohandas Karamchand, 5
Gandhi, Priyanka, 15–16, 92, 116, 125
  entry in politics, 16
  performance, 16
Gandhi, Rahul, 11, 14, 49, 121, 124
Gandhi, Rajiv, 6, 34–36, 45, 49, 105
  assassinated, 45, 49
  prime ministership, 35

Gandhi, Sanjay, 104
Gandhi, Sonia, 6, 15, 49, 66
Ganges, all-India symbolism, 7
'*Garibi hatao*', 26, 73. *See also* Gandhi, Indira
GDP growth rate, 4
General strike in Indian Railways, 30
'*Goongi gudiya*'. *See* Gandhi, Indira
Grand Alliance, 26, 83, 101
'Great leader' fascination with, 2
'Guest house incident', 109. *See also* Mayawati
Gujarat riots (2002), 59, 65
Gujral, Inder Kumar, 6, 48–50
Gupta, Sourabh, 4

Hazare, Anna, 76–79. *See also* Anna movement
Hegde, Ramakrishna, 55
Hindi-speaking parts of India, 5
Hindu card, 53
Hindu-Muslim fault line, 12, 123
Hindutva, 42, 64, 66, 68, 102, 117
History of coalitions, 1, 18
Hudson Institute, 4
Human bomb, 45

Ideological clarity, 68–69
India Against Corruption (IAC), 77
'*Indira hatao*', 26

Indo-Pakistan war (1971–72), 29
Indo-US nuclear deal, 69, 72
Industrial growth, 29
Inflations, 29
Infusion of cash in political system, 90
Interim budget, 12

Jain Commission report, 49
Jan Lokpal Bill, 77
Jana Morcha, 36
Jana Sangh, 25–26, 28, 30–31, 35, 47, 52–53, 102–4, 106
Janata Dal (Secular), JD(S), 89
Janata Dal (United), 10, 65, 84, 87–88, 101, 118
-BJP alliance, 118
Janata Party, 2, 31–33, 35, 37, 39, 42, 52, 55, 104
Janata regime, diverse orientation, 33
Jayalalithaa, J., 57–58, 82, 84, 120
Joblessness, 6, 12

Kamaraj, K., 21
Kar seva, 41
Karunanidhi, K., 121
Kashmir Valley, crackdown in, 13, 17
Kejriwal, Arvind, 77–78, 80, 83
Kesri, Sitaram, 49
Kumar, Nitish, 10, 55, 62–63, 65, 84, 87–88
Kumar, Shanta, 108

Land ceilings, 24
Leadership clashes, 69

Left Democratic Front (LDF), 84
Liberation Tigers of Tamil Eelam (LTTE), 45
Limaye, Madhu, 104
Lohia, Ram Manohar, 22
Lok Dal, 31, 37, 42
Lok Sabha elections, 87, 97, 104
Lokpal Bill, 77
Lord Ram, all-India symbol, 7

Mahagatbandhan. *See* Grand Alliance
Mahatma Gandhi National Rural Employment Guarantee Act (MGNREGA), 68, 73
Mandal and Mandir, 44, 106–8
Mandal Commission, 39–40
Mandal, B.P., 39
Mandalization of politics, 49
Maran, Dayanidhi, 91
Mayawati, 10, 16, 92, 108–12, 125
Mishra, Shripati, 105
Modi wave, 112
Modi, Narendra, 2, 6, 9, 63, 83 84–89, 92, 97–98, 125–26
  instincts, 12
  -led campaign, 81
  -Shah-led BJP, 118
Modi, Nirav, 91
Mukherjee, Shyama Prasad, 52
Muslim interests, 12

Naidu, Chandrababu, 57, 86

Narayan, Lok Nayak Jayaprakash, 30
Narayanan, K.R., 57
Nath, Kamal, 11
National Agenda for Governance, 60
National Conference (NC), 123
National Democratic Alliance (NDA), 11, 55, 58–67, 70–71, 80, 85–88, 121–23. *See also* Vajpayee, Atal Bihari
National Front, 37–39, 41, 43, 46
'National mood', 82
Nationalist Congress Party (NCP), 73, 119
Nehru, Jawaharlal, 5, 15, 18, 21–22, 69, 101
Nehru-Gandhi dynasty, 18, 69, 101
Non-BJP voters, 15
Non-Congress Actors, 37–43
Non-Congress votes, 20

Pal, Jagdambika, 110
Palampur resolution, 41
Patel, Chimanbhai, 39
Patnaik, Naveen, 39, 55, 62
Patwa, Sunder Lal, 108
Pawar, Sharad, 73
Peoples Democratic Party (PDP), 83, 123
-BJP alliance, 83
Personality-oriented campaign. *See* Vajpayee, Atal Bihari
Phoolan Devi, 105
Polarization, 56, 125
Political forces, coalition of, 32

Populism, 26, 73
Pre-election alliance, 58, 61
Prepoll arrangements, 52
Presidents' rule, 83, 103, 109, 111
Pulwama attack, 14, 87, 125
Putin, Vladimir, 14

Raja, A., 91
Rajagopalachari, C., 24
Rajya Sabha, 6, 88
Ram mandir agitation, 12, 41, 46, 53, 56, 60, 107, 111, 116–17
Ram, Jagjivan, 31–32
Ram, Kanshi, 108
Ramdev, Baba, 77
Rao, Chandrasekhar, 86
Rao, K. Chandrasekhar, 86
Rao, N.T. Rama (N.T.R.), 37, 57
Rao, P.V. Narasimha, 4, 6, 46, 49
Rashtriya Janata Dal (RJD), 10, 39, 65, 84, 88, 96, 101, 118
-Congress alliance, 88
Rashtriya Lok Dal (RLD), 42, 69, 113
Rashtriya Swayamsevak Sangh (RSS), 25, 52–53, 60, 77, 101
Ravi Shankar, Sri Sri, 77
Reddy, Jagan Mohan, 86
Reddy, Y.S. Jagan Mohan, 86
Reddy, Y.S.R., 86
Reddy, Y.V., 4
Regional identities, 50
Regionalization of the electorate, 81
Religious polarization, 45
Republican Party of

India, 102

Revolving-Door politics, 102–3

Right to Information (RTI), 73, 77

Right-wing economic policies, 25

Right-wing parties, 13

Samajwadi Party (SP), 10, 15, 39, 43, 69, 72–73, 75, 96, 101, 108–9, 111–13, 116–18
-BSP alliance, 116–17

Samyukta Vidhayak Dal (SVD), 102

Sangh Parivar, 77

Scindia, Jyotiraditya, 35

Scindia, Madhavrao, 35

Secular victimhood, 11

'Secular' mobilization, process of, 10

Shah, Amit, 63, 84–89, 97–98

Shastri, Lal Bahadur, 6, 21, 30

Shekhar, Chandra, 6, 42–43, 104–5, 107

Shekhawat, Bhairon Singh, 108

Shiromani Akali Dal (SAD), 55, 65, 85, 123

Shiv Sena, 59, 61, 63, 73, 83, 85, 87, 119

Singh, Ajit, 43

Singh, Charan, 24, 31–32, 37, 42–43, 102–4, 113

Singh, Kalyan, 104, 107–8, 110

Singh, Manmohan, 2, 4, 6, 15, 66–67, 72, 126

Singh, Rajnath, 111

Singh, V.P., 6, 35–42, 105–7

Singh, Vir Bahadur, 105–6
Single-party rule, 2, 5, 11, 63
Sruthijith K.K, 4
Stalin, M.K., 121
State-specific forces, 37–38
State-specific parties, 37
Swatantra Party, 24–26, 102

Telangana Rashtra Samithi (TRS), 65, 85–86, 100
Telugu Desam Party (TDP), 37, 39, 57, 63, 65, 85–86, 100, 120
vs. YSR Congress, 100
'Thakurvaad', 118
Third Front, 43, 47–48, 50, 52
Third Front Politics, experiment in, 47–50
Tireless campaigner. *See* Modi, Narendra
Tiwari, N.D., 104–6
Trinamool Congress (TMC), 66, 72–74, 82, 84, 96, 122
Tripathi, Kamalapati, 103
Trump, Donald, 98
2G spectrum scam, 91. *See also* Raja, A.

Uniform civil code, 60
United Democratic Front (UDF), 84
United Nations Human Rights Council (UNHRC), 75
United Progressive Alliance (UPA), 4, 15, 17–18, 66–69, 71–74, 76–78, 80, 91, 96, 121–23

Upper-caste
hegemony, 42
resentment, 45
vote, 117

Vajpayee, Atal Bihari, 2, 6, 11, 28, 35, 48, 51–63, 66, 68–70, 88, 97, 125–26
Vishva Hindu Parishad (VHP), 41, 101
Vote banks, 12, 16, 56, 60
Voter blocs, 40, 50, 73, 96, 117
Voter sentiment, 20

Workable Coalition, 113–14

Yadav, Akhilesh, 39, 92, 112
Yadav, Lalu Prasad, 10, 39, 62, 65, 84, 87, 107. *See also* Ram temple agitation
Yadav, Mulayam Singh, 10, 39, 42, 104, 107–11, 117. *See also* Ram temple agitation
Yadav, Ram Naresh, 104–5
Yadav, Sharad, 88
Yadav, Tejashwi, 39
YSR Congress Party, 86, 100, 120